Kids of All Ages

BIG BOOK of Easy-to-Do Bible Talks

DAVID C COOK

transforming lives together

BIG BOOK OF EASY-TO-DO BIBLE TALKS FOR KIDS OF ALL AGES
Published by David C Cook
4050 Lee Vance Drive
Colorado Springs, CO 80918 U.S.A.

Integrity Music Limited, a Division of David C Cook
Brighton, East Sussex BN1 2RE, England

ISBN 978-0-8307-7243-8

The content included in this book was originally published in *The Big Book of No-Object Object Talks* in 2007 © Gospel Light, ISBN 978-0-8307-4358-2.

Cover Design: James Hershberger

Printed in the United States of America

5 6 7 8 9 10 11 12 13 14

111124

Contents

Praising God

Prayer

Salvation

Seasonal

Serving Others

Showing God's Love

Telling Others about Jesus

Thankfulness

Introduction

Why This Book

In this book, you'll find 100 Bible talks that require no preparation. These talks are designed to be easy-to-do sermons for children's worship service or as part of an adult service. When you open the book to one of these Bible talks, you will not have to hunt for supplies. You only need to have kids! Simply read through each talk, and then go for it.

Additionally, included with each talk is a "Going the Extra Mile" page of activities. This is a supplement to each talk and is geared toward older children. You'll need paper and pencils or markers for these lessons and sometimes a few extra supplies. These additional lessons are designed to provide an opportunity for more in-depth discussion. It's recommended that these additional activities be led by small-group leaders to further engage children in Bible discussions.

If you are a children's pastor, encourage parents to use these Bible talks in their role as spiritual teachers of their children. Share these Bible talks with parents by photocopying the talks to give as handouts, or scan and e-mail to them.

Choosing Volunteers

These Bible talks rely heavily on asking children to volunteer. You'll want to think through what kind of child you want volunteering for certain tasks. If it's a simple task, like holding your arms in the air, you may want to choose a younger child. If the task is something fairly theatrical, a more exuberant child would be the right choice. Try not to pick the same children over and over again. Make sure to give many different children the opportunity to participate.

When choosing volunteers, you may have one or more children who will consistently raise their hands to answer questions and share their thoughts every time. You may see a child raise a hand who has never shared an idea with the class. If this happens, don't be afraid to invite the child to share his or her ideas or answers. When you ask different children to share their thoughts, their level of confidence increases and they will be more likely to participate in future discussions and activities.

With some tasks in this book, a child will need to be chosen ahead of time. This is because certain Bible talks rely on the ability of the child to do the task correctly. Other tasks require the child have a little time to think over what to do and how to do it. Of course, every group of children is different and you'll know which talks best suit your group. Right now you may have several children who are willing do anything at any given moment. So you may not feel the need to ask anyone to volunteer ahead of time. If your current group is a little more reserved, take that into consideration when choosing volunteers for Bible talks.

Questions and Answers

You'll find that these Bible talks and activities are full of questions. Most of the questions are open-ended. Here are some tips when asking these types of questions:

1. Try not to critique the children's answers. If a child's answer does not apply to the question asked, smile and say, "Thank you, Joshua" or "How interesting!" If the answer is wrong, you could say something like, "That's a good try. Who else

has an answer?" When children believe that their answers to questions will result in hurt feelings or embarrassment, very few hands will go up.

2. Be sure not to overpraise an answer. Once children sense you've found the "right answer," it is less likely other children will volunteer their thoughts. A simple "Good answer. Does anyone else have an answer?" will acknowledge the child's response and leave room for more answers to be given.

3. Some of the questions in this book are fairly simple. You may want to consider choosing younger children to answer these questions. By doing this, you help build a young child's self-confidence to continue participating. However, more challenging questions should be directed to older children. Be sure to give them time to think about their answers. When in front of a large group, children may be more reluctant to respond as quickly as they would with a smaller group.

Attitude Makes a Difference

Your attitude makes a difference in these Bible talks. The energy you put into a talk will be mirrored by the children you teach. If you're subdued and unsure, you can count on them feeling the same way. If you're filled with confidence and excitement, they'll be engaged and ready to participate when asked.

Making It Your Own

Feel free to use your own instincts and adjust whatever you wish to make these Bible talks work for you and your group of children. If you don't like the way a question is worded, change it. If you think your group of children would respond better if an activity was conducted another way, do it. The more you can make each lesson your own, the fresher and more natural each Bible talk will seem.

Finding What's Age Appropriate

When presenting a children's sermon or some type of Bible talk, most of us probably have a group of children with a wide range of ages. You might have children ages 3 to 11 years old sitting in front of you. With such a large age span, there's probably no way to completely get the point across to every child. Some lesson objectives may seem more obvious to older children but need more explanation to the younger ones. Some talks will have an impact on younger children but will not interest the older ones. Hopefully, most of the talks teach everyone something. Perhaps the same lesson will introduce a younger child to a Bible story, while teaching an older child a deeper Bible truth. Even the "Going the Extra Mile" activities, designed for third through sixth graders, have a very wide audience to reach.

Learning Styles

Not everyone learns the same way. Over the years, educators have categorized ways people learn into "learning styles." A snapshot of different learning styles among children may look something like this: Anthony likes to talk about his thoughts and feelings. Isabella prefers to actively experience what she's learning. Maddie prefers to be creative with her thoughts and ideas, while other children like Daniel love to listen to a teacher tell Bible stories. Jasmine just likes to learn new things, while Isaiah must relate to a life application before showing interest in a lesson. God made each of us different in this way. This book will offer something for every learner.

When it comes to your own learning style, "Know thyself" is appropriate. We all tend to teach the way we learn. Maybe you like to tell stories, so you need to keep that in mind and avoid telling too many of them. Knowing the way you like to learn can help remind you to keep the right balance of engaging different learning styles when teaching. You can also balance your approach to accommodate different learning styles by varying the ways you conduct activities and discussions.

The Element of Surprise

One of the most fun things about teaching children is the element of surprise. When we ask children questions, or ask them to act out something or demonstrate an idea, the results can be wildly different from what we expected. Sometimes the best learning comes when the unexpected happens. It's kind of like hiking along a mountain trail. It might be a little risky, but the view can be spectacular! Some of us don't dare ask questions or try anything new or unusual. This may be due to a fear of losing control of the children. Don't worry if the answer to your question is off the wall, or if the children all crumble into a heap laughing at each other making silly faces. It's all part of the grand surprise! Have fun while you lead children closer to Jesus!

Leading a Child to Christ

One of the greatest privileges of serving in children's ministry is to help guide children to become members of God's family. Pray and ask God to prepare the kids you know to understand and receive the good news about Jesus. Ask God to give you the sensitivity and wisdom to communicate effectively and to be aware as opportunities occur.

When talking with children about salvation, use words and phrases they understand; never assume kids understand a concept just because they can repeat certain words. Avoid symbolic terms that will confuse literal-minded thinkers. As you watch and pray, you will see kids developing relationships with God.

Here are some questions you can ask and things you can discuss with a child who is interested in accepting Jesus as their Lord and Savior. Encourage the child to look up and read the Bible verses along with you.
Read John 3:16. **Why did God send Jesus to earth?** (God loved us so much that He wants us to have eternal life with Him.)

First John 3:1 says that God wants us to be His children. But sin, doing wrong, separates us from God. Read Romans 6:23. **What do you think should happen to us when we sin?** (die) **But what is God's gift to us?** (eternal life in Jesus)

Jesus willingly died on the cross to take the punishment for our sins. Read 1 Corinthians 15:3. **But Jesus didn't stay in the tomb. After three days, He came back to life! Jesus died so that we can live forever in heaven with Him.**

Are you sorry for the wrong things that you've done? If you are, what should you do? Read 1 John 1:9. **Our sins are wiped away when we're truly sorry for what we've done and when we turn to God.**

Read Ephesians 2:8. **How are we saved?** (by God's grace, through faith) **Christian faith is a life-long adventure here on earth. With Jesus as Lord of our lives, we build a life of submitting to God, following Jesus, and keeping in step with the Spirit.**

At this point, continue to talk with the child about accepting Jesus as Lord and Savior. Include what your church teaches about how this happens. If you have any questions about salvation, talk with your pastor or children's ministry leader.

God wants every person to accept the free gift of eternal life that He's offering. What do you need to do about this?

All in the Family

God's family can work together to accomplish His commands.

Bible Talk

Everyone stand up, and while keeping one foot on the floor, try to see how far you can reach to the side with your other foot. Allow time for students to complete the task. **Trying to reach very far by yourself is pretty hard. But how far do you think we could reach if we work together to make a line that starts right here by this _________** (name a nearby object)**?** Allow time for students to tell predictions. **Let's see how far we can actually reach.** Have a volunteer begin the line by touching the object and standing with feet spread apart. Have other students come up one at a time and extend the line. Students remain connected by making sure that their feet are always touching. After all students are connected, check to see if they were able to reach their goal.

There are always things we can do by ourselves, but some things can only be done or can be done even better with the help of other people. That's how it is in God's family. Ecclesiastes 4:9 says, "Two are better than one, because they have a good return for their labor." This verse reminds us that working together can accomplish more than doing something by yourself.

What are some examples of times that God's family can work together to obey God's commands? (help people in need, be kind to a visitor at church, give money to help a missionary)

Conclusion

I'm glad we have many people who can help us obey His commands. We're all in God's family together!

Close in prayer.

Ecclesiastes 4:9

Two are better than one, because they have a good return for their labor.

Going the Extra Mile

Activity

Today, let's see how it feels to work together to help each other out of a tangle. Divide the class into groups of six to eight students each. **In your group, stand shoulder to shoulder in a circle, facing inward. Now hold hands and then tangle your circle without letting go of each other's hands.** Students may step over hands, move under raised arms, etc. **Now see if you can get untangled without letting go of each other's hands. Remember to work together and help each other accomplish the goal.** Allow time for students to untangle themselves. Repeat the activity as time permits.

Bible Discussion

The Bible tells us a story of some people who worked together to accomplish a goal. Have a student read Nehemiah 3:1–4 aloud. Let that student know there are many unfamiliar names in these verses and not to worry about pronouncing them correctly. They could even just say the first initial. **These people were all working together to build the wall around the city of Jerusalem. Because they all worked together, they were able to accomplish their goal. Even when it was hard, they kept working together.**

- **What choice did all these people have to make? What could they have done instead?**

- **When have you worked on a project with another person? How did it feel when you accomplished your goal?**

Life Challenge

Working with other people can be hard sometimes. We might have different ideas of how to do something. But when we help each other out, it makes a big difference in how we are able to follow God's commands.

Prayer

Lord, we praise You for giving us people who can help us follow Your commands. Please help us to see when we can help others too. In Jesus' name. Amen.

Brothers and Sisters in God's Family

We are all brothers and sisters in the family of God.

Bible Talk

How many people are in your family? Allow time for several children to answer. **Let's see how fast you can form some new "families."** Ask children to stand up and begin walking in a circle or walking randomly around the room. Call out a number between three and five. Children will see how fast they can form "families" of that number. When all families have formed, encourage each family member to give a high five to their new brothers and sisters. Depending on the number of children, some families may need to "adopt" an additional family member. Repeat the activity as time permits, each time calling out a different number. It's fun to think about what it would be like to have new brothers and sisters.

Our real families are all different, but there is one family we all can be part of—God's family, the church. These words came from Jesus Himself. He said in Matthew 12:50, "Whoever does the will of my Father in heaven is my brother and sister and mother." Jesus is saying that everyone who loves Him is part of the family of God.

Conclusion

As members of the family of God, we are all brothers and sisters. That means even though we may argue with each other from time to time, we can love and rely on each other as brothers and sisters would.

Close in prayer.

Matthew 12:50

Whoever does the will of my Father in heaven is my brother and sister and mother.

Going the Extra Mile

Activity

Sometimes the people who live in a family have a hard time getting along with each other. What are some of the things that people in a family might argue about? Allow time for several children to give answers.

Since we know God wants family members to do their best to get along and live in peace with each other, let's see if we can come up with the top ten ways to live in peace and resolve conflicts. Help students form groups of three to six. Groups will work together to make lists of ways to live in peace with brothers and sisters in a family. After several minutes, ask groups to share their lists. After all lists have been shared, lead children to determine the overall top ten suggestions.

We might wish that we never had any arguments with the people in our families, but part of living in any family is learning how to get along with each other. You've come up with some great ideas!

Bible Discussion

The people who live in God's family have to learn to get along with each other and live in peace too. Let's look at Acts 6:1–7 to find out what happened when some people in God's family had to figure out a way to live in peace and resolve a conflict. Have a student read the passage aloud.

- **Who was involved in this conflict? What was the conflict about?**
- **What were the choices God's family made to resolve the conflict? What choices could they have made instead?**
- **What were the results of their choice to resolve this conflict peacefully?**

Life Challenge

Our church families are important because our church family is God's family. God wants us to act like a close, loving family of brothers and sisters when we are at church. Sometimes we may have conflicts, but God will help us resolve our conflicts as we love and care for each other.

Prayer

Lord, You have given us the gift of a family right here at church. Show us how to live as brothers and sisters who love You and love each other. Help us to resolve conflicts in ways that please You. In Jesus' name. Amen.

Instruments of God

We all have different abilities God uses to accomplish His plans.

Bible Talk

Who here plays a musical instrument or can imitate the sound of a musical instrument? Great! When I point to you, make the sound of the instrument that you play or that you can imitate. Allow time for as many volunteers to participate as possible. **The sound of a single instrument is great, but you know what I really love is a good orchestra or band. In an orchestra or band, several instruments are playing at the same time to make beautiful sounds. Could you imagine a band with no guitar or an orchestra without a trumpet? Each instrument is important in order to make good music.**

Our church is similar to an orchestra or band. Each of us is different but a very important part of the church. The preacher is very important, but so are the ushers, the music leader, and the children too. Paul said it very well in 1 Corinthians 12:14, "The body is not made up of one part but of many." Paul understood that God made all of us very special and important to the whole body of the church.

Conclusion

We all need each other to have a great church and to share the love of Jesus with others.

Close in prayer.

1 Corinthians 12:14

The body is not made up of one part but of many.

Going the Extra Mile

Activity

Help students form groups of three to six. **In your groups, I would like you to create your own band. Together, your group can choose the instruments you'd like to have in your band. Each person in your group can choose an instrument to play. All at once, each person will make the sound of the instrument they chose to play and act out playing the instrument. Let's make a band!** Allow time for groups to form their bands. Invite groups to have their bands "play" for the larger group. **You all made terrific music together!**

- **What do you think would have happened if one person didn't play his or her instrument?**
- **Was it hard or easy to play in a band together? Why?**

Bible Discussion

In Paul's letter to the church in Corinth, he explained the importance of every member in the church. Have a student read 1 Corinthians 12:14–20.

- **Based on these verses, what is a church supposed to believe?**
- **When is a time our church has worked together to show our love for God or others?**

If we want to follow Jesus, then we need to use our gifts and abilities to help others learn about Jesus. Just like your band needed each person to play an instrument, our church needs to use everyone's special talents and work together to share God's love.

Life Challenge

God gave us all different abilities to share with one another. We can use our abilities at church, at school, and at home. If we ignore one person's abilities, it's harder for us to accomplish God's plans.

Prayer

Lord, thank You for giving each of us special abilities. Help us to appreciate each other's abilities and use them to share the love of Jesus with others. In Jesus' name. Amen.

Learn from Your Elders

Younger Christians can learn from older Christians.

Bible Talk

I would like each older child (third grade and up) **to go sit beside one or two younger children.** (Use ages appropriate for your group.)

If you are an older child, what is something you can do to help the younger child by whom you are sitting? What might you help him or her learn to do? Allow several older children to respond.

If you are a younger child, what do you want to do when you are older? Allow time for several younger children to respond.

As we grow, we are able to learn new things from people who are older than us. The Bible tells us that young people can look up to and learn from older people. The Bible also sometimes calls older people "elders." Elders have the responsibility to guide and care for younger Christians. First Peter 5:2 says, "Be shepherds of God's flock." Every Christian is a part of God's flock. The Bible uses the word *flock* to describe us, like a flock of sheep. And every flock of sheep needs a shepherd to care for them. The elders at our church are just like shepherds who protect and care for younger Christians like you.

Conclusion

So today—and every day—look for the good things you can learn from Christians who are older than you. And remember that kids younger than you are watching you to learn ways of following God.

Close in prayer.

1 Peter 5:2

Be shepherds of God's flock.

Going the Extra Mile

Activity

Let's have the older kids stay seated next to the younger kids for this activity. Older kids are going to teach a secret handshake to the younger kids next to them. Allow time for older kids to make up any kind of handshake and teach it to younger kids around them. Invite younger children to share what they learned. **Excellent job! How did it feel to learn something new from your older friends?**

Bible Discussion

The first Christians knew how important it was for older Christians to teach and be a good example for younger Christians. Have a student read 1 Peter 5:1–5 aloud.

- **What does Peter say the actions of elders, or older Christians, should be like?**
- **Why do you think Peter tells elders to be like shepherds? How do shepherds care for their sheep?**
- **What might a kid your age do to help a younger child learn how to follow Jesus?**

Peter knew that in order for the early church to grow, younger Christians had to be willing to learn from older Christians. They both had to be loving and kind when they were together.

Life Challenge

We can all learn new things from older Christians about being followers of Jesus. God wants us to be willing to learn and be obedient to our elders. As we all care for each other, we'll learn from each other and grow as Christians.

Prayer

Lord, thank You for everyone in our church family. Help us to learn from our elders. Show us ways we can teach others. In Jesus' name. Amen.

One Language

Even people who speak different languages can all believe in Jesus.

Bible Talk

I'm going to say *hello* in four other languages. First, I'll tell you the words and then you can tell me if you think the word is French, Italian, Chinese, or Spanish. After reading the words, allow some time for answers.

Ni hao (NEE-hah-ow) Chinese

Hola (O-lah) Spanish

Bonjour (bohn-JOOR) French

Buongiorno (bwuhn-JOOR-noh) Italian

People in our world today speak so many different languages. It's too bad that we all can't speak one language so that we all can understand one another.

In the Bible, there is a story of how people from all different nations understood each other. One day, Christian leaders began to speak about Jesus to a big crowd of people. In that crowd were people from many countries. The Bible says that each person understood what was being said. Sometimes this day is called the Day of Pentecost. It must have been fantastic for everyone to understand the good news of Jesus and have an opportunity to believe in Him.

Conclusion

I have some good news for you today too. We may not be able to understand what a person from China or Kenya or Iran says; but no matter what language a person speaks, if the person believes in Jesus as Savior, we can share and understand our love for God. Read Philippians 2:10–11 aloud.

Close in prayer.

Philippians 2:10–11

At the name of Jesus every knee should bow ... and every tongue acknowledge that Jesus Christ is Lord.

Going the Extra Mile

Activity

I'll need two volunteers for this activity. Choose two volunteers. **I'm going to whisper a task to one volunteer.** Whisper a task to the first volunteer (sharpen a pencil, get a Bible, jump three times, clap ten times). Without speaking or writing words, and without doing the task, the first volunteer will try to get the second volunteer to do the task. Allow a few minutes for the two volunteers to communicate the task.

- **Because you couldn't use words, how did you communicate your ideas?**
- **How would being able to use words have made your job easier?**
- **What are some things that are easy to communicate without words? What kinds of things are hard to communicate? Why?**

Bible Discussion

Let's take a closer look at the story in Acts about the Day of Pentecost. Have a student read Acts 2:1–13 aloud.

- **What was surprising about this story?**
- **How did God help people hear the good news about Jesus and believe in Him?**

On that amazing day, people from all over the world could hear and understand the message of Jesus in their own languages. God's Holy Spirit made it possible for these people to communicate. Some people refused to believe what they heard. They claimed the Christians must have been drunk. The Bible tells us that many people, however, did choose to believe in Jesus.

Life Challenge

As Christians, we can share our love for God and our belief in Jesus as Savior with people all over the world.

Prayer

God, thank You for people all over the world. Show us how to share our love for You no matter what language we speak. In Jesus' name. Amen.

A Way of Escape

When we are tempted to do wrong, God promises to help us escape by saying no to temptation.

Bible Talk

Let's find out how many things you have in common with each other. Everyone, think of your favorite flavor of ice cream. When I give the signal, start walking around the room, saying your favorite flavor aloud. When you find someone who likes the same flavor, stand next to each other and wave your hands in the air. Give the signal, and allow time for students to complete the activity. Quickly name the students who have in common a fondness for a certain ice cream flavor. As time permits, repeat the activity with other items (favorite pets, favorite sport, eye color, etc.).

We all like different things, but there are some things we have in common with others too. The Bible tells us that there is something we ALL have in common. We are all tempted at one time or another to disobey God—to sin. First Corinthians 10:13 says, "No temptation has overtaken you except what is common to mankind." This verse means that the wrong things I've been tempted to do are also the same wrong things you or other people have been tempted to do. The good news, however, is that 1 Corinthians 10:13 also says, "When you are tempted, he will also provide a way out so that you can endure it." God promises that He will make a way for us to resist the temptation and will help us do what is right.

Conclusion

Every day we make choices about the things we say and do. When we think about the choices we make, we might be tempted to disobey God and sin. But for every temptation, remember that God will give you a way of escape. He'll help you obey!

Close in prayer.

1 Corinthians 10:13

When you are tempted, he will also provide a way out so that you can endure it.

Going the Extra Mile

Activity

Place a large sheet of paper and markers on a table or on the floor. Students should stand around the edges of the paper. **When I say "Go," start walking around the paper. When I say "Stop," get a marker and write on the paper a Bible command.** Lead students in the activity, allowing time for students to write or draw situations. Suggest commands as needed, although commands can be repeated. **Now we're going to play this game again. But this time when you stop, read the command on the paper in front of you and try to think of a situation in which kids your age can choose to obey the command. Write or draw the situation.** Lead students to complete the activity. Then invite volunteers to tell commands and situations. **God doesn't promise that we'll never be tempted to disobey, but He does promise to help us say no to the temptation.**

Bible Discussion

The Bible tells us that even Jesus, God's Son, was tempted to do wrong. We can find out what Jesus did when He was tempted. Have a student read Matthew 4:1–11 aloud.

- **What did the Devil tempt Jesus to do?**
- **What did Jesus do to say no to these temptations? How did God's Word help Jesus?**
- **When are kids your age often tempted to do wrong? What have you learned from God's Word that would help in those situations?**

One of the ways God helps us escape from temptation and say no to doing wrong is by giving us the Bible. When we read and pay attention to what the Bible says, it helps us make the right choice.

Life Challenge

When we are tempted to disobey God, it can be hard to remember that God is with us and will help us. Sometimes we just want God to take away the temptation. But God has promised to help us—by giving us the Bible, and by giving us parents or teachers who can encourage us to obey Him. There's always a way of escape!

Prayer

Dear God, thank You for being with us and for providing a way of escape for us when we're tempted to disobey You. Help us to rely on You. In Jesus' name. Amen.

Do What It Says

God's Word shows us what Christians should be like.

Bible Talk

Today we're going to play a mirror game. I would like each of you to get a partner and stand facing your partner. Allow time for students to find partners. If needed, pair up with a student so each child has a partner. **Now choose one person to do an action such as wave hands, walk in place, make a face, or swing arms. The other person tries to mirror, or copy, the action.** *(Optional: Demonstrate the activity with a partner.)* Allow a few minutes for students to complete the activity, and then have partners switch roles.

Great job! You knew how to act by imitating your partner's actions. In the same way, we learn how to act as Christians by imitating the actions we read about in God's Word. James 1:22 says, "Do not merely listen to the word, and so deceive yourselves. Do what it says." As Christians, we can mirror the instructions given to us in the Bible.

Conclusion

When we mirror our actions after what the Bible says, we don't just listen and read about what God says in His Word—we begin to do what it says.

Close in prayer.

James 1:22

Do not merely listen to the word, and so deceive yourselves. Do what it says.

Going the Extra Mile

Activity

Today we'll play a game of charades. Charades is a game in which players act out something so that others can guess what they're acting out. Help students form groups of three to six. Give each group one or more Bibles. **I'm going to give each group a Bible verse that describes to us what Christians should be like. In your groups, you'll act out the Bible verse for another group to guess what command your Bible verse tells about. For example, if your group has a Bible verse about kindness, your group would act out a way someone might show kindness.** Assign one of the following Bible verses to each group. Allow time for students to find and read verses and decide how to act out a way someone might obey the verse.

Psalm 100:2—"Worship the Lord … with joyful songs."

Proverbs 17:17—"A friend loves at all times."

Romans 12:13—"Share with the Lord's people who are in need."

Galatians 5:13—"Serve one another humbly in love."

Colossians 3:13—"Forgive as the Lord forgave you."

1 Thessalonians 5:17—"Pray continually."

James 1:19—"Everyone should be … slow to become angry."

Bible Discussion

When Jesus lived on earth, He told a story about the results of obeying God's commands. Have a student read Matthew 7:24–27 aloud.

- **What did Jesus say the foolish man did? What about the wise man?**
- **What is someone like who does not obey God's Word?**
- **In your own words, what would you say is the main idea of these verses?**

Paying attention to God's Word and putting His commands into practice will help us build lives that are strong. Even when things happen that make us worried or sad, we'll be able to depend on God.

Life Challenge

God's Word tells us everything we should know about living as His followers. When we do what God's Word says, we show others what Christians are like and how God intended His followers to live. When others see our actions, they can be inspired to become God's followers too!

Prayer

God, thank You for Your Word—the Bible. Help us to do what Your Word says we should do. In Jesus' name. Amen.

Hiding God's Word

Memorizing and thinking about God's Word helps us remember to love and obey Him.

Bible Talk

What is something you've memorized? Allow time for several volunteers to come forward and repeat a poem, a nursery rhyme, words of a song, a cheer, or an advertising slogan. **Good job! You've all done a lot of memorizing!**

The Bible talks about memorizing God's Word. Psalm 119:11 says, "I have hidden your word in my heart that I might not sin against you." What do you think it means to hide God's Word in our hearts? Allow students to respond. **To hide God's Word in our hearts means to memorize God's Word so it will never leave our minds. In the same way we memorize poems or rhymes or songs, we can memorize God's Word. The more we read and think about and memorize God's Word, the more it will help us love and obey Him.**

Conclusion

We can depend on God's Word to give us the strength to obey! With God's Word in our hearts, we can show our love for God by obeying Him.

Close in prayer.

Psalm 119:11
I have hidden your word in my heart that I might not sin against you.

Going the Extra Mile

Activity

Write each phrase of Psalm 119:11 on a separate sheet of paper. Repeat phrases as needed so there is a sheet of paper for each student. Hide the sheets of paper around the classroom. **I have hidden parts of our Bible verse, Psalm 119:11, on several sheets of paper around the room. When I say "Go," I would like everyone to stand up and look around the room to find a sheet of paper. After you've found a sheet of paper, see if there is anyone else who has the same phrase. Then line up so that the words of the verse are in the correct order. Ready? Go!** Students can find papers and line up in verse order. Lead students in saying the verse aloud. Repeat the game as time permits, allowing volunteers to hide the papers for each round of the game.

Bible Discussion

Jesus told a story that helps us learn how important it is to read and pay attention to God's Word. Have a student read Matthew 13:3–8 aloud.

- **What happened to the seed that fell along the path? The seed that fell in rocky places? The seed that fell among thorns? The seed that fell on good soil?**

Have a student read Matthew 13:18–23 aloud.

- **What did Jesus say happens to the person who receives the Word of God along the path? The person who receives the Word of God in rocky places? The person who receives the Word of God among thorns? The person who receives the Word of God on good soil?**

- **What would you say is the main point of this story?**

- **What is one way that you can be like the good soil?**

Life Challenge

When we memorize God's Word and pay attention to what it says, it helps us to grow as Christians and remember ways to love and obey God. Let's thank God for giving us His Word.

Prayer

Dear God, thank You for giving us Your Word. Help us to memorize Your Word and to do what it says. In Jesus' name. Amen.

Learning about God

We can learn about God's greatness by reading the Bible.

Bible Talk

We learn many things about the world in different ways. What would you expect to learn if you read a math book? Allow a few volunteers to tell examples of math problems. **What would you expect to learn if you read a science book?** Allow a few volunteers to tell examples of science facts. **What would you expect to learn if you read a history book?** Allow a few volunteers to tell examples of historical facts. **What would you expect to learn if you read the Bible?** Allow a few volunteers to answer.

We can learn about God when we read the Bible. When we read the Bible, we find out who God is, what makes Him so great, and why He created our world. Just like a math book helps us learn about math, the Bible helps us learn about God.

Conclusion

The Bible is often called "God's Word" or the "Word of God" because in it He tells us everything we should know about what God is like. Job 36:22 says, "God is exalted in his power. Who is a teacher like him?" When we read the Bible, God teaches us about Himself. The Bible is God's book for us.

Close in prayer.

Job 36:22
God is exalted in his power. Who is a teacher like him?

Going the Extra Mile

Activity

Help students form groups of three to six. Give each group a Bible, paper, and pens or pencils. Assign each group one of the following verses, repeating verses as needed: Genesis 1:1; Joshua 1:9; Psalm 24:1–2; 46:1; 103:2–3; 1 John 3:1. **In your group, read the verse(s) you have been assigned. On your paper, write the reference you read and what you learned about God. Try to answer the questions: What is God like? What does He do?** Allow time for groups to complete the task. *(Optional: As time permits, groups trade papers with each other so that they can read additional verses.)* Ask a volunteer from each group to tell what the group learned about God.

Bible Discussion

Long ago, in Bible times, a man named Elijah helped many people learn about God. Elijah was a prophet, which meant that he told people messages from God. When God's people were worshipping a false god named Baal, Elijah challenged the prophets of Baal to a contest. Let's find out what happened. Have a student read 1 Kings 18:22–24, 26–29, 36–39.

- **Who won this contest? How?**
- **What did the people learn about God from this contest?**
- **What are some other ways God has shown His power and that He is the one true God?**
- **When we read the Bible, we can explore and learn amazing and wonderful things about God.**

Life Challenge

Every day this week, try to learn something new about God by reading the Bible. You can choose to read a Scripture passage every day or read a Bible story you learned about in church. The more we read about God, the more we understand Him.

Prayer

God, thank You for the Bible. Help us to read the Bible every day so we can learn more about You. In Jesus' name. Amen.

The Best Way to Live

God gives His Word to us so we will know the best way to live.

Bible Talk

Raise your hand if you think you could walk across the front of this room with your eyes closed. Have a student who responds try to complete the task. Be available to steer the student if needed. As time permits, allow several students to try. **If you've seen the place you're trying to walk to, you might be able to make it safely with your eyes closed.**

If you've never been to a place before, what do you need to help you walk there safely with your eyes closed?

In order to walk safely through unfamiliar places, we need someone to guide us. Have students come forward, line up facing the same direction, and place hands on the shoulders of students in front of them. All students except the first student in line should close their eyes. The first student leads the line of students on a curving path across the room. As time and interest permit, allow several students to have the opportunity to be leaders. *(Optional: Depending on the space and the number of students, you may wish to have three or four lines of students moving at the same time.)* **Having a guide or leader who knew where to go sure made a big difference in being able to walk safely and confidently!**

Psalm 119:105 tells us God's Word is like a guide or leader. This verse says, "Your word is a lamp for my feet, a light on my path."

When do you most need a lamp or a light? (when it's dark, when you don't know where you're going)

Conclusion

The stories we read in the Bible and the commands from God all help us know the best ways to live. God's Word is the guide we can all depend on!

Close in prayer.

Psalm 119:105
Your word is a lamp for my feet, a light on my path.

Going the Extra Mile

Activity

Help students form groups of three to six, and give them paper and pencils. **In your group, pretend to be the designers of a web page. Your job is to design a web page entitled "What's So Great about the Bible?" With the people in your group, talk about what should be on your web page that will explain what everyone should know about the Bible and why it's so important. Your web page should let people know the benefits of reading God's Word. Some of your group can draw pictures too.** Give groups eight to ten minutes to design their web pages. Then allow some or all of the groups to show and describe their work.

The Bible is God's true story, and reading it not only helps us know and love Him; it helps us know the best way to live.

Bible Discussion

Let's find out some reasons why the Bible is the best guide for our lives. Have students take turns reading Psalm 119:9, 11, 18, 35, 89, 103–104.

- **How is God's Word described in these verses?**
- **According to these verses, how does God's Word help us?**
- **What can kids your age do to get to know what's in God's Word?**

There are always going to be times when we're not sure what to say and do. When we need a guide or leader, we can depend on God's Word and the people God gives us to help us learn about His Word.

Life Challenge

The more we know about what is in the Bible, the better we can understand and obey God's commands. Each of us needs a guide or leader to help us know the best way to live. God has given us the perfect guide!

Prayer

Lord, thank You for giving us the Bible. Help us make time every day to read and think about Your Word. Remind us to let Your Word be our guide. In Jesus' name. Amen.

A Not-So-Hopeless Situation

God can give us hope, no matter how many tough situations we may face.

Bible Talk

Ask all students to stand. **If you like to play basketball, pretend to dribble and shoot a basketball. If you like to play football, pretend to catch a football and do a touchdown dance.** As time permits, repeat the action for other sports (soccer, baseball, swimming, etc.).

If a group of professional athletes in any of these sports came into the room, do you think you would have any hope of beating them? Why or why not?

You might feel hopeless if you had to play against a professional athlete.

What does it mean to feel hopeless?

Feeling hopeless is awful! It can make us feel like giving up. The good news is that with Jesus we can always have hope. Think of some sad or angry times when you have felt like giving up. No matter what tough situations we're in, God promises to give us hope. Jeremiah 29:11 tells us God's promise to give us hope. Read Jeremiah 29:11 aloud. **We all go through tough times when we're sad, angry, or confused. Sometimes we feel like giving up, but God promises us that there is hope in our future.**

Conclusion

God always keeps His promises, and He will always help us. With God we can always have hope!

Close in prayer.

Jeremiah 29:11

I know the plans I have for you ... plans to give you hope and a future.

Going the Extra Mile

Activity

Help students form groups of three to six. **In your groups, try to give me three answers to the question: When might a child your age feel hopeless? Then decide what you would say to a child so he or she might have hope in the situation.** Give groups several minutes to list answers. Then ask groups to share their lists. Discuss the lists by asking the following questions:

- **How might God help a child in one of these situations?**
- **If you have a friend who is having a tough time and feeling hopeless, what might you say or do?**

Bible Discussion

Even in the worst situations, God gives us hope. Let's look at a sad story in the Bible, when hope was found even in the worst of situations. Have a student read Acts 7:54–60 aloud. **Stephen knew he was about to be killed. Yet as he was being killed, he had hope! He prayed for Jesus to receive his spirit, and even found it possible to forgive those who murdered him. Stephen had hope, because he knew that he was going to be with Jesus in heaven.**

Life Challenge

If Stephen can find hope as he faced death, surely we can find hope in whatever we might be facing. Think of a problem you're dealing with right now. Maybe it's a kid at school you just can't get along with. Maybe your schoolwork just seems too hard. Maybe something difficult is happening in your family. As we get ready to pray, think about something you need God's help with right now. I'll give you a few moments to say a silent prayer for the situation you're in. Ask God to help you find hope as you face that challenge.

Prayer

Allow a few moments of silence for students to pray in their hearts. **Lord, You are the giver of hope. Thank You for giving us hope in difficult times. We know that as long as You are with us, we will always have hope. In Jesus' name. Amen.**

Don't Worry

When we feel worried, we can remember to trust in God.

Bible Talk

Let's play a memory game about things we trust will work. I need everyone to stand in a big circle. Help students form a large circle. **In this game, we'll go around the circle and name things we trust will work every day. Listen closely to what everyone says, because when it's your turn, you will try to say what the people have said before you. For example, if I took the first turn, I would say, "I trust in my car." The person who goes after me would say, "I trust in my car and my TV." We will continue the game until the last person has repeated what everyone has said plus added one last response. Ready to play?** Begin the game yourself and lead students in playing. For younger children, lead them to name up to five items before beginning a new round.

In our game, we named things that we trust will work. But do these things ALWAYS work? Allow time for several students to answer. **What might keep a car from working? How about a flashlight? How about a marker or pen?**

The Bible tells us about trusting in God. John 14:1 says, "Do not let your hearts be troubled. You believe in God; believe also in me." This verse tells us that when we are worried, we can remember to trust—believe—in God. The great thing about God is that we can ALWAYS trust Him. There is never a time when He won't love us, hear our prayers, and help us know what to do.

Conclusion

We all have days when we feel like we don't have any problems or unhappy things in our lives. But on those days when you're worried about a problem at school, or a friend does something that makes you feel sad or upset, remember that God is with you every single day. You can trust in Him to give you what you need.

Close in prayer.

John 14:1
Do not let your hearts be troubled. You believe in God; believe also in me.

Going the Extra Mile

Activity

Help students form groups of three to six. **I will assign each of your groups a place kids your age often go.** Assign each group one of the following places: home, church, school, friend's house, amusement park, campground.

In your groups, discuss what a kid your age might worry about in the place your group was assigned. For example, what would a kid your age worry about at an amusement park? Allow time for groups to discuss. Invite groups to share what they discussed. **In all these situations, ask God for help and remember that you can trust Him to help you know what to do and to provide people who will care for you.**

Bible Discussion

When Jesus lived on the earth, He talked to a huge crowd of people about times they might worry. Let's find out what He said. Have a student read Matthew 6:25–34 aloud.

- **Why does Jesus say we should not worry?**
- **What does Jesus say about the birds of the air?**
- **What does Jesus say about the flowers of the field?**
- **What does Jesus say we should do in verse 33?**

When we seek God's kingdom, it means we show by our words and actions that we love God and want to obey Him. God promises we can trust Him to help us have the things we need.

Life Challenge

In the Bible, Jesus tells us we don't have to worry. In our activity today, you discussed places where kids your age might worry about something. It doesn't matter where we are; God is always with us and wants us to trust He knows what's best for us.

Prayer

Father God, thank You for always being with us. Help us to trust in You and not worry. In Jesus' name. Amen.

Fear Factor

We can rely on God to be with us and help us through our fears.

Bible Talk

How many of you have been to the zoo and have seen the lions? They sure are fierce animals. They're big and strong with the loudest roar you've ever heard. Who can demonstrate a great big lion's roar? Invite several volunteers to demonstrate roars. **Those roars were awesome. They scared me, and I knew you weren't really lions.**

In the Bible, we can find a great story about a man named Daniel, who had to stay all night long in the same place with a bunch of lions. Here's what happened. One day King Darius made a law that anyone who prayed to a god or man except the king would be put in a lions' den (probably like a cave). Daniel was not about to stop praying to God. So he was thrown into a den of lions to be eaten. Do you think Daniel was scared? You'd better believe he was! But he knew God would be with him no matter what happened. The next morning the king went to check on Daniel. To his surprise Daniel was alive and well! Daniel said, "My God sent his angel, and he shut the mouths of the lions" (Dan. 6:22). **After that, the king was convinced Daniel's God was the one true God.**

Conclusion

We'll all face fears in life. But we can learn from the story of how Daniel handled his fears. He faced his fears knowing that no matter what happened, God would be with him. God promises His help when we're afraid. Read Isaiah 41:10 aloud. **We can remember to have faith that God is with us and is ready to help us, no matter what fears we face. Whether it's a mean kid at school, the dark, or an illness, rely on God to be there to face your fear with you.**

Close in prayer.

Isaiah 41:10

Do not fear, for I am with you.

Going the Extra Mile

Activity

Help students form groups of three to six. **Think of a scary situation you or someone you know has been in. Tell your group the story.** After everyone has told a story, have the small groups report a scary story to the large group.

- **What makes a situation scary?**
- **How can trusting in God help?**
- **What do you know about God that helps you trust Him?**

Bible Discussion

We've already taken a quick look at the story of Daniel and the lions' den. Let's take a closer look at what happened to cause Daniel to get into so much trouble. Have a student read Daniel 6:1–17 aloud. **Daniel did everything the right way. He became the king's most trusted adviser. But because of evil men, he ended up with the choice to betray God or face death. Daniel's fear could have caused him to run from God, but he decided to trust in God. He chose to face death.**

- **If you were Daniel, what would you have done?**
- **Why do you think Daniel chose to depend on God?**

Life Challenge

Being a follower of Jesus can bring us face-to-face with our fears, just as it happened with Daniel. We won't be able to face our fears unless we put our trust in God like Daniel did. Sometimes our fear tempts us to ignore God. We can resist that temptation and rely on God's help. He promises to help us know what to do, even when our fears are as scary as being in a lions' den! Invite a volunteer to read Isaiah 41:10 aloud.

Prayer

God, thank You for giving us strength when we are afraid. Help us to trust in You when we are afraid. Thank You for taking care of us in a world that can be so scary sometimes. In Jesus' name. Amen.

God Will Help You Speak

When we aren't sure what words to say for God, He will help us.

Bible Talk

Let's pretend for a moment that for some reason the pastor can't be here today. Raise your hand if you would be willing to preach a sermon. If any students raise their hands, ask them what they'd preach about. Ask the rest of group why they wouldn't want to preach. **Preaching sounds like a scary idea, doesn't it? Fortunately, our pastor is here today and prepared to preach a sermon.**

In Bible times, Moses considered himself to be a very poor speaker, but God wanted him to lead the Hebrew people and speak for them to the mighty Egyptian pharaoh. Moses didn't think he could do it. But listen to what God told him in Exodus 4:12: "Now go; I will help you speak and will teach you what to say." God reassured Moses that he could handle the task given to him if he would only depend on God. We can all be ready to speak for God, and we can depend on Him to guide us in the right things to say.

Conclusion

There will often be times when God will want you to say something for Him. For example, there might be a time you can remind someone of God's promises, or tell someone about God's love. We can remember that God will help us know what to say.

Close in prayer.

Exodus 4:12
Now go; I will help you speak and will teach you what to say.

Going the Extra Mile

Activity

Help students form groups of three to six. **In your groups, read the Bible verse I assign you. Then think of and plan how to act out a situation showing a way to obey the verse.** Assign each group one of these verses: Psalm 47:6; 107:1; Proverbs 13:10; Mark 11:24; Colossians 3:20.

Allow a few minutes for students to complete the task. Have groups act out situations for the class. **Terrific work! We can ask God for help, and He will give us the right words to say and the right actions to do.**

Bible Discussion

Let's take a closer look at Moses and how God led him in what to say. Have a student read Exodus 4:10–17 aloud. **Moses was scared about what God had asked him to do. He kept making excuses. God told Moses to trust He would give him the right things to say. Eventually, after even more excuses, the Lord allowed Moses to take his brother Aaron along to help him speak. Finally, Moses did what God wanted him to do and was able to eventually lead the Hebrew people out of Egypt.**

- **When might a kid your age feel scared like Moses?**
- **What do you know about God that will help you when you are afraid to do something right?**
- **Who has God given to help you?**

Life Challenge

We all will have times when God wants us to speak out for Him, and like Moses, we won't want to. Just remember to have faith that God will help you say and do the right thing.

Prayer

God, help us to have the right words to say, and give us the right actions to do. Thank You for choosing us to speak for You. In Jesus' name. Amen.

Learning from Our Leaders

God gives us leaders who teach us how to love and obey Him.

Bible Talk

Have students stand in a circle. **Let's try a wave circle. A wave circle is when one person starts a wave by moving his hands like an ocean wave.** Demonstrate a wave motion. **The person who starts the wave is the leader. Once the leader starts the wave motion, everyone else follows the leader's actions, one at a time. We continue the wave motion until everyone in the circle has had a chance to do the motion. Who would like to be our leader?** Choose a volunteer and decide which direction the wave will go. **Let's start the wave circle.** The volunteer starts the wave circle by initiating a wave motion. Give help as needed to continue the wave motion around the circle. **Wonderful!** Repeat the wave circle activity as time and interest permit, choosing a different leader each time. *(Optional: Students can see how fast they can make the wave motion.)*

The leaders in our game instructed us on what to do to in the wave circle. Without the leaders, we would not have known when or how to start the wave circle. Just like we needed leaders to play this game, we need leaders to know the best ways to love and obey God. Psalm 32:8 says, "I will instruct you and teach you in the way you should go; I will counsel you with my loving eye on you." This verse means God wants to teach us ways to love and obey Him. One of the ways He does that is by giving us leaders at church, at home, and at school.

Conclusion

Think about the people God gives to be your leaders. Pay attention to the ways they act, and listen to what they say. Every day try to learn something about how to live in the very best way.

Close in prayer.

Psalm 32:8

I will instruct you and teach you in the way you should go; I will counsel you with my loving eye on you.

Going the Extra Mile

Activity

Divide the class into two equal groups. The first group forms a small circle in an open area of the room. The second group forms a larger circle around the first group. **To play this game, each circle is going to walk in the opposite direction. For example, students in the smaller circle walk clockwise, and students in the larger circle walk counterclockwise.** Allow time for groups to practice walking in opposite directions. **When I give the signal, walk in your circle. When I say stop, stop walking and find the person in the other circle who is standing closest to you. That person will be your partner. Face your partner and take turns telling each other the name of a leader who teaches you how to love and obey God. This leader could be a Sunday school teacher, a pastor, your parents, or anyone else who teaches you to love and obey God.** Lead students to play the game as time permits.

Bible Discussion

Let's look at a story in the Bible about a man named Joshua. We can find out how he became a leader. Have a student read Joshua 1:1–2, 5–7 aloud.

- **Who do you think taught Joshua to love and obey God?**
- **What did Moses teach Joshua?**
- **What did God command Joshua to do?**

God taught Joshua how to love and obey Him. One of the ways Joshua learned about obeying God was from Moses. Because Joshua learned from Moses, he was ready to lead the Israelites into the promised land.

Life Challenge

When Moses first started teaching Joshua about God, Joshua probably didn't know that one day he would be the leader of God's people. We don't know what God might want us to do in the future either. But every day, as we learn from people how to love and obey God, it helps us be ready to do the good things God wants us to do. Let's thank God for the leaders He gives us.

Prayer

God, thank You for giving us leaders. Help us learn from our leaders ways we can love and obey You. In Jesus' name. Amen.

Needs or Wants

We can depend on God to give us everything we need.

Bible Talk

I'd like everyone to stand and find a partner. Allow time for students to find partners. If needed, be a partner with a child. **Now follow me and do this clapping pattern.** Demonstrate the clapping pattern as you describe it. **First, tap your thighs. Then clap your hands and then tap the palms of your partner, before clapping hands and tapping your thighs again.** Allow time for partners to practice.

Now, as we repeat this pattern, when you tap your partner's hands, each of you say out loud something kids your age WANT to have. Think of a few things ahead of time. Give partners time to repeat the pattern enough to name at least three or four items. **Now, when you tap your partner's hands, each of you say out loud something kids your age NEED to have.** Give partners time to name at least three or four items. **Thank you!** Have students sit down.

What were some of the wants and needs you heard people say? Allow time for students to respond. **Sometimes we get confused and think that our wants are things that we really need. We may think, I really need that new toy. But do we really need it, or do we just want it?**

Of course, it's fun to think about the things we want. But it's also good to remember that God knows what we really need and will help us have what we need. Jesus said in Matthew 6:8, "Your Father knows what you need before you ask him." God may not always give us what we want, but He knows what is best for us and will always give us what we need.

Conclusion

Because God loves us, we can depend on Him to help us have the things we need.

Close in prayer.

Matthew 6:8
Your Father knows what you need before you ask him.

Going the Extra Mile

Activity

Let's play a game like Pictionary to help us think about the differences between the things we want and the things we need. Have a volunteer come forward and start drawing something he or she thinks is a need or a want. Other students try to guess what the item is. After each item is guessed, have students discuss whether they think it is a need or a want. Repeat the activity as time permits.

Bible Discussion

Jesus told a big crowd of people about why they can depend on God to meet their needs. Let's see what He said. Have a student read Matthew 6:25–32 aloud.

- **What are some of the ways God shows His care for birds and plants?**
- **What did Jesus say about God's care for us?**
- **When is a time a kid your age needs to remember God's care?**

Jesus wanted us to know that our needs will be met. God takes care of the plants and animals, and He'll surely provide us with what we need.

Life Challenge

The next time you think about something you want, try to decide whether it is a want or a need. Then remember God loves you and will help you have the things that are best for you—whether they are wants or needs!

Prayer

Lord, thank You for Your love. We praise You that we can depend on You to take care of each and every one of us. In Jesus' name. Amen.

A Real Gift

Jesus is God's gift to the world.

Bible Talk

I need three volunteers. Choose three volunteers to come to the front of the room. **Let's suppose I have a gift for every volunteer. You tell me if you think the volunteers really received gifts. Let's pretend I gave _________** (name a girl student) **a gift.** Pretend to give a gift. **Then I tell her that the gift will cost her $5. Is that really a gift? Why?** Allow a few volunteers to answer.

Let's pretend I gave _________ (name a boy student) **a gift.** Pretend to give a gift. **Then I ask him to return the gift to me in two days. Is that really a gift? Why?** Allow a few volunteers to answer.

Now suppose I give ___________ (name a girl student) **a gift.** Pretend to give a gift. **Then she says, "I don't want your gift." Is that really a gift? Why?** Allow a few volunteers to answer. **What is the only way for someone to truly receive a gift?** Allow a few volunteers to answer.

God offers His Son, Jesus, as a gift to the world. Romans 6:23 says, "The gift of God is eternal life in Christ Jesus our Lord." This verse tells us God gave Jesus to us as a gift so we could believe in Him and have eternal life.

Conclusion

God must have thought we were pretty special to give us an incredible gift like Jesus! When we believe in Jesus, we accept God's gift to the world. Jesus is a free gift; we don't have to pay to accept Him, nor will God ask for His gift back. Jesus is a gift everyone can have!

Close in prayer.

Romans 6:23

The gift of God is eternal life in Christ Jesus our Lord.

Going the Extra Mile

Activity

I'm going to pass out a sheet of paper to everyone. I'd like for you to draw one of the best gifts you've received in your life. This could be a gift you received on a holiday or a gift you received on another occasion. Distribute paper and markers. Allow time for students to complete the task and show their drawings. **It's fun to receive gifts. All of us have received different gifts, but Jesus is a gift each of us can receive. We can thank God for sending Jesus to be a gift to the world.**

Bible Discussion

Let's read about why Jesus is such a wonderful gift to the world. Have a student read Matthew 1:18–22 aloud.

- **Based on these verses, what important task was Jesus born to do?**
- **What did Jesus do to show that He was God's Son?**
- **What words would you use to describe Jesus?**

Jesus was sent from God to save people from their sins. Because He never sinned, Jesus was the only one who could do this important task.

Life Challenge

When we choose to believe in Jesus, we accept God's greatest gift to us. God wants us to accept His gift, but He will never force us to accept it. If you have never received this gift, you can accept it today. And even better, you can tell others about the gift God has given to the world.

Prayer

God, thank You for Your gift to the world. Help us to share the good news of Your gift with others. In Jesus' name. Amen.

God Is on Our Side

Because of God's great love for us, He is on our side.

Bible Talk

Let's play ball! We're going to mimic playing a baseball game. I need four volunteers to be in the game. Assign volunteers a position in the game (first baseman, second baseman, third baseman, and pitcher). *(Optional: Choose more students to play additional positions like catcher, center field, right field, left field, and umpire.)* **I will need one volunteer to be a batter and mimic hitting a home run. Choose one volunteer. Everyone else can be fans who will cheer as loud as they can for the batter.** After all positions are chosen, have kids stand in position in an open area of the room. Have fans positioned at the side of the room or against a wall. **Time to play ball!** Have the pitcher pitch an imaginary ball and have the batter imitate swinging a baseball bat. *(Optional: Use a soft ball to play the game or use objects around the room to create bases.)* **Looks like a home run!** Have the batter run around the bases, scoring a home run. **What a great game! The fans are cheering wildly!** *(Optional: Repeat the game with new students playing each position.)*

Although it may seem like the biggest participation in the game came from the players, the fans in our baseball game had an important job too. They showed their support for the batter by cheering. Cheering for someone is a way people show they are on someone's side or they support the person. God supports us in the same way. Because of His great love for us, He is on our side. The Bible tells us in Romans 8:31, "If God is for us, who can be against us?" This verse does not mean our baseball team will always win or we'll always win any contest. But it does mean God can help us do our best.

Conclusion

It doesn't matter who wants us to fail; when God is on our side, He is like our personal fan! He's always cheering for us and helping us no matter what situation we are facing.

Close in prayer.

Romans 8:31
If God is for us, who can be against us?

Going the Extra Mile

Activity

Help students form groups of three to six. Pass out large sheets of paper and markers or crayons. **In your groups, create a cheer to help us remember that God is on our side. For example, "God, God, He roots for me, He helps me get to victory!"** Allow time for students to create one or more cheers. Invite students to share their cheers.

Bible Discussion

Listen to these verses that help us discover more about what it means to know that God is on our side. Have a student read Romans 8:31–39 aloud.

- **What are the things God does to show He is on our side?**
- **What do you learn about God's love in these verses?**
- **When might a kid your age need to remember these verses?**

Life Challenge

Because God loves and cares for us, we can depend on Him for many things—to forgive our sins, to protect us, to give us courage, and to help us know the best things to do in any situation. This week, remember the cheers of your number one fan!

Prayer

Father God, thank You for being on our side and cheering for us! Thank You for Your love that is stronger than anything. In Jesus' name. Amen.

Just the Way You Are

God loves us just the way He created us.

Bible Talk

It can be so much fun to pretend to be someone else. We can put on makeup or wear a costume to pretend to be someone different. Think about someone you'd like to pretend to be. Stand up, and on the count of three pretend to be that person. Allow time for the children to think. **Ready? One, two, three!** Children should demonstrate and act. **I see lots of great pretending. Thank you. Please sit down.**

That was a lot of fun! But have you ever tried to pretend that you were sad so that people would feel sorry for you? Or have you tried to pretend that you were really smart? Maybe we pretend to be silly so people will like us. Or maybe we pretend to be tough so people will think we're brave and strong. Or perhaps we act glamorous so people will think we're cool.

When are some times kids your age might pretend to be something they aren't?

How do you feel when you are pretending to be something you aren't?

There are lots of reasons why we might pretend to be something we aren't. But when we remember that God made us, we don't have to pretend to be someone or something else. We can just be what

God made us to be. No pretending necessary! Psalm 139:14 says, "I praise you because I am fearfully and wonderfully made." That means we don't have to try and act a certain way so people will like us.

Conclusion

Knowing God made us in a wonderful way helps us realize we can just be ourselves—the amazing people God made us to be!

Close in prayer.

Psalm 139:14

I praise you because I am fearfully and wonderfully made.

Going the Extra Mile

Activity

I need some volunteers who like to act to come up to the front. I'm going to ask each volunteer to act out a certain type of attitude, and the rest of you will guess what attitude they are acting out. Choose four volunteers. One at a time, whisper to a volunteer how you want him or her to act. Assign one attitude to each volunteer:

- Silly
- Cool
- Tough
- Aloof (don't care)

Give each of the children about 15 seconds to act out their assigned attitude, and then see if the other children can guess the attitude.

- **Why do some kids pretend to be silly?**
- **Does pretending to be cool help you make friends?**
- **Why might a kid your age want to be tough?**
- **How do you feel about someone who is aloof?**

Bible Discussion

The Bible tells a story about a young man who discovered he couldn't pretend to be something different. What do you remember about the story of David and Goliath? We know that young David, armed with only a sling and five smooth stones, defeated the giant Goliath. Let's look and see what King Saul tried to make David wear before the fight. Have a student read 1 Samuel 17:38–40 aloud.

- **What did King Saul want David to pretend to be?** (a fierce soldier)

But David discovered he didn't need to pretend to be anyone else. David knew all he needed was his sling, some stones, and faith in God.

- **If David had chosen what King Saul wanted, what might have happened?**

Life Challenge

David faced a big challenge in confronting Goliath. He could not have defeated him any other way except by being the person God made him to be. That's the only way we can win when we face challenges too. We can proudly be who God made us to be!

Prayer

Lord God, we praise You for making each of us the way we are. Help us to act just the way You made us, and not any other way. In Jesus' name. Amen.

Loved No Matter What

No matter what abilities you have or don't have, God loves you unconditionally.

Bible Talk

Everyone, stick your tongue out and try to touch your nose. Give children 10 to 15 seconds to try it. Encourage the children as they work at it. You may even want to try it yourself! **That was a good effort. Who was able to do it? Great job! I guess God gave some of us the ability to touch our noses with our tongues. Being able to touch your nose with your tongue is a funny ability to have! Each of us, however, has other abilities that help us do important things.**

What abilities do some kids your age have?

God loves us all the same, no matter what abilities we have or don't have. God loves those who aren't good at sports just as much as He loves those who are. He loves people who can't sing just as much as He loves people who can. People who aren't straight-A students are loved by God just as much as those who are straight-A students. Psalm 100:5 says, "The Lord is good and his love endures forever." That means that God's love is with us forever, no matter what we're good at or not so good at. Now that's an amazing kind of love, isn't it?

Conclusion

We don't have to worry about whether we'll be good enough for God's love. It is with us forever.

Close in prayer.

Psalm 100:5

The Lord is good and his love endures forever.

Going the Extra Mile

Activity

Pass out paper and pencils or pens to every student. **Think of someone famous whom you really admire. Draw a picture of that person. Then beside the picture, list all the reasons why you think that person is cool.** Give the children five to seven minutes to complete the task. Older children or adult helpers may help younger children write their lists. When everyone is done, let some of the children share their work. Remember not to judge their choices for whom they admire or why. **Thanks so much for your work!**

If God were to make a list of reasons of why He loves you, the list would be a mile long. Hold up a blank piece of paper. **But even if there were nothing on the list, God would love you in a tremendous way. Because you see, God doesn't love you for what you can or can't do. He loves you because He created you. He thinks you're priceless and wonderful no matter what.**

Bible Discussion

When Jesus chose His disciples, He proved that God loves us no matter what. Have a student read Matthew 4:18–22 aloud. **Jesus needed to find some men to help Him tell everyone about God. You would think He would have looked for very smart men. Maybe He would have looked for men who were very wealthy to help fund His work. Or perhaps Jesus would have gone to the temple to find religious leaders to help Him. No, Jesus chose a bunch of fishermen. Fishermen usually made very little money, and they definitely weren't religious leaders. But Jesus loved them and they loved Him, and that was all that mattered. Because He knew they would love and obey Him, that made them good enough to be His disciples.**

Life Challenge

Jesus chose His disciples not based on what they could do, but based on His love for them. That's what's so amazing about God's love. He loves us before we even love Him. It doesn't matter how cool, smart, or talented we are.

Prayer

Lord God, we thank You for loving every one of us no matter what. Thank You for giving each of us special abilities to share with others. In Jesus' name. Amen.

Loving the Unlovable

God loves everyone the same, even those who are difficult to love.

Bible Talk

Before the sermon, ask an older child to be ready to tell a short, well-known story (such as The Three Little Pigs or Goldilocks and the Three Bears). Tell the child he or she won't have to tell the whole story. Let the child know that while telling the story, you will be distracting the audience. **I've asked __________** (name of a child chosen) **to come and tell us a story. Let's all listen to the story.** While the volunteer tells the story, sit among the other children and do annoying things (laugh at odd times, take your shoes off, rub the child's head next to you, make a funny sound, etc.). After a minute, thank the volunteer. ___________ (name of child chosen) **did a great job telling the story, but what was wrong with what I did?** Allow several volunteers to answer. **You're right! I was rude and disrespectful.**

I acted that way as a reminder of how difficult some people can be. I bet you know kids who are just really hard to like. They might do all kinds of annoying things! Being friends with them seems like a real challenge sometimes. But guess what? Jesus loves them just as much as He loves you and me. And He wants us to love them too! Read 1 John 4:11 aloud. **There's a great story in the Bible about a tax collector named Zacchaeus. People disliked him because he cheated people out of their money. But when Jesus came to town, He decided to go to Zacchaeus's house. Everyone was shocked! How could Jesus hang out with such a terrible guy?**

Jesus was showing that He loves everyone and we should love them too. Because Jesus showed Zacchaeus love, Zacchaeus changed his cheating ways.

Conclusion

If we show love to those who are hard to love, maybe they'll change their ways too. Jesus wants us to try!

Close in prayer.

1 John 4:11
Dear friends, since God so loved us, we also ought to love one another.

Going the Extra Mile

Activity

Everyone, close your eyes and use your imagination. Let's pretend you have moved to a new school. You quickly discover that everyone thinks the way you dress is funny. They think the way you talk is weird. They dislike the TV shows you like. The jokes you think are funny, other children think are boring. Every time you say something, the rest of the children just shake their heads in disgust. You are the most disliked student in class. Think for a moment how you would feel. Allow a few seconds of silence.

A miserable week has passed at your new school. Suddenly one day, while you're eating your lunch alone, two of the other kids at school sit down beside you. At first you think they're there to play a joke on you. But instead, they ask you how you like your lunch. Then you begin to talk about different things like homework, teachers, and pets. The two children are very friendly to you. Think about how you feel now. Allow a few seconds of silence. **In a few weeks, these new friends who have been so kind to you ask you to come to their church. Now think about whether or not you will go with them to church.** Allow a few seconds of thought. **You can open your eyes now.**

- **Why do you think the two kids were so kind to you?**
- **Why do you think the other kids were so mean?**
- **When are some other times kids your age need people to be kind?**
- **Why might it be hard to be kind when others are being mean?**

Even when it's hard, we can remember that God's love is for everyone. When we show His love, it helps others learn about God's love. Our kind actions can make a big difference in someone's life!

Bible Discussion

Let's talk some more about the time when Jesus was kind to Zacchaeus. Have a student read Luke 19:1–10 aloud.

- **How were Jesus' actions different from the actions of the people in the crowd?**
- **What were the results of Jesus' actions?**

When no one else cared about Zacchaeus, Jesus cared! What a difference Jesus' love made in his life! Zacchaeus paid back everyone he'd stolen from and gave them back four times what he had taken. That means if he stole $10 from them, he gave back $40. Then he gave half of his possessions to the poor—all because Jesus showed him love.

Life Challenge

We can ask Jesus to help us love the unlovable. Every day look for opportunities to show God's love to others, even when it might be hard. We never know whose life Jesus may change because we showed His love.

Prayer

Lord, thank You for Your love. We know You love everyone. Help us to love others, even when it's hard. In Jesus' name. Amen.

No Condemnation

We can show that God's love does not condemn but shows mercy.

Bible Talk

Today we're going to talk about what bugs us, or bothers us, the most about other people. Have the students stand in a circle. **Starting with** ___________ (name any student), **we're going to spell out the word *bugs* with each person saying one letter of the word. Whoever says the letter *S* can finish one of these sentences: "It really bugs me when somebody …" or "I really don't like it when somebody bugs me by …"** After going around the circle a time or two, ask students to mix up their places in the circle and repeat the activity. Continue as time permits, or until each student has had a turn to complete a sentence.

There are always going to be times when other people bug us or do things we think are wrong. Sometimes it's easy to condemn others because of what they do. To condemn someone means to judge someone, to call them guilty. But God wants us to show His love and be merciful. Luke 6:36 says, "Be merciful, just as your Father is merciful." When we show mercy, we love and forgive someone, even when the person doesn't deserve it. That's how God treats us, and He wants us to love others in the same way.

Conclusion

We can recognize the wrong actions of others and help them stop doing wrong, but still show we care about them. God can help us show mercy instead of condemnation.

Close in prayer.

Luke 6:36

Be merciful, just as your Father is merciful.

Going the Extra Mile

Activity

Help students form groups of three to six. Give each group several index cards and pencils. **In your group, write brief descriptions of situations in which kids your age might condemn others for their wrong actions.** Help students think of situations as needed. Examples: a friend who frequently lies, a kid at school who cheats on tests, a kid in the neighborhood who is in a gang, etc. After students have written situations, collect all the cards. Place the cards facedown on the floor in rows. A volunteer from each group takes a turn to toss a coin onto the rows of cards. The volunteer turns over the card on which the coin lands (or the nearest card) and reads the situation aloud. Students tell a way to respond to the situation that shows mercy and love.

Bible Discussion

When Jesus lived on earth, He gave some good examples of ways to show mercy to others. Let's find out what He said. Have a student read Luke 6:27–36 aloud.

- **What are the examples of merciful actions Jesus describes?**
- **Which of these actions would be the hardest to do? Why?**
- **How would your school or neighborhood be different if people obeyed Jesus' commands?**

Even though we know others have sinned, these verses don't limit the kind of people to whom we show love and mercy. Instead of worrying about others' sins and condemning them, we need to make sure we've confessed our own sins to God. Then we can receive His forgiveness and help so we can obey Him—showing others the same kind of love we've received from Christ.

Life Challenge

Think of one person you know whom others may condemn. Ask God to give you courage to be a friend and show mercy.

Prayer

Lord, thank You for loving us and showing us mercy, even when we sin. Help us to love others the way You love us. In Jesus' name. Amen.

Second Chances

Because of God's love, He forgives us when we sin.

Bible Talk

Let's see if we can say a tongue twister together. First, listen to me as I say the tongue twister. Repeat the following tongue twister several times, and then invite students to say it with you. **A big black bug bit a big black bear that made the big black bear bleed blood.** Then invite a few students to try repeating the tongue twister on their own. If time permits, students can say other tongue twisters they know and have the group try to repeat.

Raise your hand if you needed more than one try to get the tongue twister right. Allow students to respond. **Saying tongue twisters is fun. But we almost always need a second or third chance—or even more chances—to say them correctly.**

In our lives, we need second chances too. We do wrong things when we disobey God. The Bible calls those wrong things sin. But because of God's great love for us, He will forgive us when we ask Him. Psalm 86:5 says, "You, LORD, are forgiving and good, abounding in love to all who call to you." God gives us a chance to start over!

Conclusion

When we sin, we might feel like God doesn't love us anymore. But it's great to know that God's love is so big He will always forgive us when we pray to Him. He's ready to help us start over and do our best in obeying Him.

Close in prayer.

Psalm 86:5

You, LORD, are forgiving and good, abounding in love to all who call to you.

Going the Extra Mile

Activity

Help students form groups of three to six. Give each student a sheet of scrap paper. Students should crumple the paper to make small paper balls. **In your groups I'd like one person to make a circle with their arms like a basketball hoop. Everyone else in the group will stand five feet away from the hoop and try to shoot the paper ball through the hoop. Let's see which group can make ten baskets first.** Let students shoot baskets. Adjust the distance students stand from the hoop as needed. After one group has made ten baskets, call an end to the game. Ask a student from the winning group to tell about a time he or she needed a second chance and did NOT receive it. Example: math problem on a test, striking out in a baseball game, etc. Repeat the game as time permits, allowing different students to be the basketball hoops. **This game reminds us to be glad and thankful that God ALWAYS gives us a second chance and more!**

Bible Discussion

In the Bible there's a story about a man named Saul, who received a second chance. Let's see what the Bible says about Saul. Have students take turns reading Acts 9:1–19 aloud.

- **What did Saul want to do to the people who believed in Jesus?**
- **What happened to Saul on his way to Damascus?**
- **What did Saul learn about Jesus and about God's love?**

Later, Saul was called Paul and did many great things for God. Saul used the second chance God gave him to tell others about God's love.

Life Challenge

Think about a time when you need to remember God's love and forgiveness. God's love isn't just for people in the Bible. God's love and forgiveness are for everyone.

Prayer

God, thank You for giving us second chances. Forgive us for the wrong things we do, and help us to follow You. In Jesus' name. Amen.

God Gives Us Strength

God gives us strength.

Bible Talk

Today we're going on a pretend journey. Is everyone ready? Then let's get started by walking in place. Lead children to walk in place with you. **We're coming up to a very steep hill. Are you ready to climb? Let's start climbing.** Lead children to make exaggerated climbing motions. **Climb up the hill farther and farther. Wow, we're really starting to get tired now.** Pretend to be tired. **But we must keep going. Climb up the hill.** Speed up the climbing motions. **Can we do it now? Let's go! Faster and faster we go.** Speed up the climbing motions. **We're almost there. We made it! Awesome job, everyone! You can sit down now.**

Climbing up a mountain is something that takes a lot of the climber's strength. Sometimes we have to do things that take a lot of strength too. Listen to what Isaiah 40:31 tells us to do when we need strength: "Those who hope in the Lord will renew their strength. They will soar on wings like eagles; they will run and not grow weary, they will walk and not be faint." What an amazing verse! God will renew our strength when we feel like we can't do something. When we need strength to study our homework, God can give us strength. When we need strength to not eat bad foods, God can give us strength.

Conclusion

No matter what we need strength for, God promises to help us!

Close in prayer.

Isaiah 40:31
Those who hope in the Lord will renew their strength.... They will run and not grow weary.

Going the Extra Mile

Activity

Give each student a sheet of paper and a pencil. **I'd like for each of you to sit quietly by yourself for a few minutes and think of a time when you needed more strength to get a hard job done. Then, on your paper, write a prayer asking God for strength the next time you're in a similar situation.** If you have some children who aren't proficient writers yet, have them draw a picture of themselves praying. After about five minutes, invite volunteers to show their pictures and read their prayers. **Sometimes we all may feel as if we don't have enough strength to get through difficult situations. We can know God will answer our prayers and give us strength.**

Bible Discussion

The Bible has many passages that tell us about God's strength. Have a student read Psalm 28:7–9 aloud.

- **What words are used to describe God?**
- **What do these verses say God will do to show His strength?**
- **What can we do to show we trust in God's strength?**

Because God is so strong, He can be a shield and a fortress of safety for us.

Life Challenge

Maybe you've had times when nothing seems to go right for you. Maybe you and your family are having a tough time. Maybe school has become very hard for you. Perhaps you don't see any way to finish a project that you started. You can ask God to give you strength to get through the situation. Remember that God never gets tired, so He'll always be there to help you.

Prayer

Lord, we need Your strength every day. There are some days we just don't think we can make it. Help us to rely on You to give us strength. In Jesus' name. Amen.

God Is Everywhere

No matter where we go or what's happening in our lives, God is with us and He never leaves us.

Bible Talk

Where do you go to find hot dog buns? Ask for a volunteer to answer. **Where do you go to find a new shirt?** Ask for a volunteer to answer. **Where might you go to find a new toy?** Ask for a volunteer to answer. **Where do you go to find God?** Ask for a volunteer to answer. You may get answers like "church" or "Sunday school." Affirm those answers. **Thanks for giving your answers.**

Now let's see what the Bible says about where we can find God. Read Matthew 28:20 aloud. **We can find God right here in church, but do you know where else we can find God? God is with us everywhere we go. God is a spirit, and because He's a spirit He doesn't have a body like ours to limit where He is. If you're at school and having a hard day, God is there. If you get sick and have to go to the doctor, God's with you. If you and a friend are playing outside, God is right there too. The Bible says God is everywhere.**

Conclusion

Jesus' promise to always be with us wasn't just true for the people in the Bible. It's true for our own lives too. So this week, wherever you are and no matter whether you're having a good day or a bad day, remember that God is right there with you.

Close in prayer.

Matthew 28:20

Surely I am with you always, to the very end of age.

Going the Extra Mile

Activity

I'm going to give each of you paper and a marker. Draw a picture of a time and place when a kid your age might wish God wasn't around. Pass out the paper and markers and give the children about five minutes to draw their pictures. Draw a picture yourself and show it to them. When they see you've been real with them, they'll be more willing to be real with you. When time is up, invite the children to share their pictures. Don't judge them or their pictures. Simply acknowledge their work and their honesty.

Bible Discussion

It sounds so wonderful to know God is everywhere, but there may be times when we really don't want God to be with us. Let's look at some people in the Bible who wished God wasn't around. Have a student read Genesis 3:1–13 aloud.

- **What choices did Adam and Eve make in this story?**
- **Why do you think they chose to disobey God?**
- **What could they have done instead?**

Adam and Eve tried to get away with what they knew was wrong. They had hoped God wasn't around and He wouldn't see their wrong actions. Of course, we know God is everywhere all the time.

Life Challenge

When we do wrong things, we may sometimes wish God wasn't around. However, we are always better off with God right there with us every moment of every day. When hard situations come up and we want to do what is wrong, that's when we need God with us the most. Because when we know God is with us, we know that we can ask Him for help to do what's right. And if we disobey God, we know that He is STILL with us. When we ask Him, He will forgive us.

Prayer

Lord, we're glad You are always with us, even in times when we do something wrong. We want to remember that You are always with us so that we'll be encouraged to love and obey You. Thank You for always being with us. In Jesus' name. Amen.

Unbreakable Promises

God's promises can never be broken.

Bible Talk

Who can think of something breakable and imitate its sound when it breaks? Allow time for several volunteers to respond. **Those were some outstanding breaking sounds!**

Now, who can tell us some things that can't break? Allow time for several students to give answers. **What we know will never be broken are the promises God makes to us in His Word.**

There will always be times when our friends and families won't be able to keep their promises. For example, your parents may have promised to take you swimming, but then it turned out to be a rainy day, so they couldn't keep their promise.

It doesn't matter what happens in our lives; we can always count on God to stay right here with us. He won't disappear or ignore us when things get tough. Joshua 23:14 says, "Not one of all the good promises the Lord your God gave you has failed." God's promises are unbreakable! We can always count on Him to give us the help we need.

Conclusion

It's so good to know that God's promises will never be broken.

Close in prayer.

Joshua 23:14

Not one of all the good promises the Lord your God gave you has failed.

Going the Extra Mile

Activity

Have students sit on chairs in a circle. One student volunteers to be "It" and stands in the middle of the circle of chairs. Remove the extra chair. **Who needs to remember God's promises?** It answers, "People wearing blue," "All the girls," or "Everyone." The students named jump up to trade chairs while It also tries to sit down on a chair. The student who is left without a chair becomes It. Repeat the game as time permits.

Between rounds of the game, ask volunteers to read aloud these Bible verses that tell promises God makes: Joshua 1:9; Psalm 23:3; Isaiah 40:8; John 14:1–3; 1 John 1:9.

No matter how young or old you are, God's promises are for you!

Bible Discussion

There's a wonderful psalm that talks about believing in the promise of God's love. Have a student read Psalm 13 aloud.

- **How does the writer of this psalm feel?**
- **When is a time a kid your age might feel sad and unhappy?**
- **What is the writer of this psalm asking God to do?**

In the first part of this psalm, the writer is going through a tough time, and he feels like God has disappeared. Then the writer of this psalm begs God to show Himself and take care of him. At the end of the passage, the writer realizes that the Lord's love is good and never-ending. He realizes God has kept His promise to be with him and love and care for him.

Life Challenge

We all have times when we are happy and excited, or sometimes sad and worried. But no matter how we might feel, we can depend on God. His promises and love for us are unbreakable!

Prayer

Lord, we praise You for loving us all the time! We thank You for Your unbreakable promises. Help us to remember Your love and care every day. In Jesus' name. Amen.

What about Guilt?

When we feel guilty because we've sinned, we can ask God to forgive us and He will keep His promise.

Bible Talk

Make a face and pose to express the emotion of excitement. **What emotion do you think I'm showing?** Volunteers can guess.

Now I'm going to call out some emotions like anger or sadness. As I call out each emotion, show me your best expression of the emotion I call out. You can use your face and your body to show the emotion. Ready? Call out some or all of these emotions: anger, boredom, frustration, excitement, sadness, jealousy, guilt. Pause after each emotion to give kids time to show the emotion. End with the emotion of guilt.

Great job! You all really know how to show your emotions. The last emotion we showed was guilt. Let's talk about some of the times that kids your age might feel guilty. What might make a person feel guilty? Allow time for students to give ideas.

When we've disobeyed God, or done something wrong, we often feel guilty. Our feelings of guilt might make us even think that our parents or God will never love us or trust us again. The Bible gives us good news, however, when we feel guilty.

First John 1:9 says, "If we confess our sins, he is faithful and just and will forgive us our sins and purify us from all unrighteousness." If we confess, or tell, God that we are sorry for our sin, He promises to forgive us.

Conclusion

Knowing about God's forgiveness is such good news. It makes us feel joy! *(Optional: Have children pose faces and bodies to demonstrate joy.)*

Close in prayer.

1 John 1:9
If we confess our sins, he is faithful and just and will forgive us our sins and purify us from all unrighteousness.

Going the Extra Mile

Activity

Help students form groups of three to six. Give each group two sheets of paper and pencils. **In your groups, use one sheet of paper to write a brief description of a situation when someone your age has done something wrong.** After several minutes, call time and collect all papers. Then redistribute the papers, making sure that no group receives its own paper. **Now, read the situation on the paper your group was given. Sometimes, in addition to asking God for forgiveness, we can do something to help make the situation right. On the blank sheet of paper, write a way someone your age could make up for the wrong situation.** Ask several groups to share their answers.

God will help us when we've sinned, not only by forgiving us but also by helping make the situation right.

Bible Discussion

All of us, even the leaders in Bible times, have sinned and need to ask for God's forgiveness. Let's find out what David, a great king in Bible times, prayed when he sinned. Have a student read Psalm 51:1–4, 10–12 aloud.

- **What words did David use to describe God?**
- **What are words David used to describe wrong actions?**
- **What did the writer ask God to do?**

David knew his sins were keeping him from following God's plans. He was asking God to forgive him and to help him love God and obey Him.

Life Challenge

None of us is perfect. We're all going to disobey God at times. When we disobey, however, God doesn't give up on members of His family. You can ask God for forgiveness any day or anytime. He's always ready to give you the joy of forgiveness!

Prayer

Lord, thank You for forgiving us when we sin. Thank You that Your forgiveness can help us feel joy. In Jesus' name. Amen.

God Is in Control

When life gets out of control, God still cares for us.

Bible Talk

Let's pretend we're all in a car together and I'm driving. Turn your back to the students and put your hands out on an imaginary steering wheel. **Everyone buckled up? Here we go. Start it up. *Vroom*! Put it in gear and off we go. Let's take a left here.** Pretend to turn the wheel left. **Everyone, lean with me. Stop sign!** Tilt your heads back. **Off we go again. Let's go faster.** Pretend to whip around curves left and right. **Oh no, I can't slow down! Watch out for that little old lady!** Pretend to swerve the wheel. **We barely missed her. I still can't slow down. We're going to crash! *Screech!*** Have everyone slump over.

That was a crazy out-of-control ride! Sometimes we get so busy with school, sports, and playing with our friends that we feel like our lives are out of control. There might be times when we get worried about what's going to happen to us. The Bible says in 1 Peter 5:7, "Cast all your anxiety on him because he cares for you." *Anxiety* is a word that describes feeling worried or nervous. When we cast our anxieties on God, it means that instead of worrying, we depend on Him to help us, care for us, and show us what to do.

Conclusion

We can remember that God always cares for us, even when we're worried and feel as though our lives are out of control.

Close in prayer.

1 Peter 5:7
Cast all your anxiety on him because he cares for you.

Going the Extra Mile

Activity

One of the best ways we can show we depend on God is by talking to Him in prayer about our worries and problems. Have students form groups of three to six. Give each group several large self-stick notes and pencils. **In your group, think of several problems kids your age might pray about. Write your ideas on separate notes.** Allow time for students to complete this task. Collect the notes and attach them in different places around the room. **Now, when I say "Go," one person from each group runs to grab a note and bring it back to that group.** Give groups a moment to choose a designated runner. **Ready, set, go!** After each group has collected a note, read each note aloud. Talk with students about the suggested problems, asking students to tell ways God might answer their prayers about the problems.

Bible Discussion

Jesus told a story that helps us learn more about how God answers our prayers. Have a student read Luke 11:5–13 aloud.

- **What do you learn about God from this story Jesus told?**
- **What do you learn about how we should act when we have problems?**

Because God knows everything about us, He knows what will be best for us. So in the times when we are worried or don't know what's going to happen, we can count on Him.

Life Challenge

We all have good things that happen in our lives, and we all have times when we are worried. It's great to know we can always pray and talk to God about our needs. He cares for us!

Prayer

Dear God, thank You for always being in control of our lives, even when we don't know what is going to happen. Help us to remember that we can count on You to be in control. In Jesus' name. Amen.

God Protects Us

God protects and cares for us in tough times.

Bible Talk

Who has seen a mother hen with her baby chicks? What do the baby chicks do when it starts to rain? Allow time for several volunteers to answer. **They run for cover under the protective wings of the mother hen. Let's all pretend we're baby chicks and it's starting to rain. First, I'd like you to spread out and walk around the room. Then when I say "Rain! Rain!" everyone move to a corner of the room for protection from the rain. Ready to play? Here we go!** Play the game several times.

You must be glad to be protected from the rain! Just like baby chicks are protected, God protects and cares for us too.

The Bible says in Psalm 61:4, "I long to dwell in your tent forever and take refuge in the shelter of your wings." God can shelter us during hard times we may face. God is able to care for us, even when someone or something threatens to harm us.

Conclusion

God is always with us to make sure we are cared for.

Close in prayer.

Psalm 61:4

I long to dwell in your tent forever and take refuge in the shelter of your wings.

Going the Extra Mile

Activity

Crumple scrap paper to make a number of small balls. Divide the class into three teams. Explain that one team will be Throwers, one team will be Protectors, and the other team will be Targets. **Let's have the Throwers and Targets make straight lines on opposite sides of the room. Protectors will line up in the middle between them. Throwers will try to throw the paper balls at the Targets, while the Protectors act like shields for the Targets. Let's play!** Play several rounds. Have teams switch roles each round. **Way to go, Protectors! You did a great job protecting the Targets.**

- **Protectors, how did it feel to protect someone?**
- **Targets, how did it feel to have people protecting you?**
- **When has someone protected you?**
- **When have you been able to protect someone else?**
- **When has God protected you or someone in your family?**

Bible Discussion

The book of the Bible called Psalms often talks about God's protection. Have a student read Psalm 61:1–5 aloud.

- **How do you think God's protection is like a rock?**
- **When might kids your age need to remember God's care and protection?**

The author of these verses needed God's protection. He describes God's protection as a rock, a refuge, a strong tower, a tent, and the wings of a mother bird.

Life Challenge

When we have tough times and we're afraid of what will happen, God will protect us. In every tough situation, we can ask God to protect our bodies and minds.

Prayer

Lord, thank You for loving us so much that You want to provide a safe place for us. Help us to depend on Your protection when we face tough times. In Jesus' name. Amen.

Coach God

We can trust God to teach us how to live His way.

Bible Talk

Let's vote on who are your favorite sports heroes, actors, and singers. Ask three volunteers to each suggest the name of a favorite sports hero. **Now when I say each name, if that person is your favorite, stand up and clap three times.** Lead children to complete the activity. Repeat the activity with favorite actors and singers.

Thanks, everyone. It looks like we all like different athletes, actors, and musicians. We like all these people because they are good at what they do. What if one of them suddenly showed up today and said to you, "I want to be your coach"? What would you say?

Would any of you say, "No, thank you, that's okay. I don't need your help"? No, of course not! You wouldn't say no to your favorite basketball star if he wanted to teach you how to shoot hoops. You wouldn't say no to your favorite singer if she volunteered to teach you how to sing. No one would pass up the chance to be coached by people who are considered the best in what they do.

Believe it or not, sometimes we turn down God's offer to help make us the best people we can be. Sometimes we say, "No, God, I don't need Your help. I can figure this out on my own." But God is the ultimate coach for how we should live. Psalm 86:11 says, "Teach me your way, LORD, that I may rely on your faithfulness."

Conclusion

We can always be ready for God to coach us in His ways. He knows better than anyone how we can live our lives the best way possible.

Close in prayer.

Psalm 86:11

Teach me your way, LORD, that I may rely on your faithfulness.

Going the Extra Mile

Activity

Coaching means you are teaching someone how to do something. Who would like to come up and teach us something you're good at? Maybe you'll want to teach us how to shoot a basketball, do a hard math problem, or braid hair. Allow time for a few volunteers to come up and coach the group in a specific task. **That was some top-notch coaching!**

- **What does a good coach need to know?**
- **What does a good coach need to do?**
- **In order for us to learn from a coach, what do we need to do?**

It doesn't matter what situation we're in, God is always there to give us direction just like a good coach would!

Bible Discussion

The book of Judges has a wonderful story about a man named Gideon who did what his coach asked, even when it didn't make sense to him. Have a student read Judges 7:2–8 aloud.

- **Why did God tell Gideon there were too many soldiers?**
- **What do you think Gideon learned about God through this story?**
- **What would you have thought if you were Gideon?**

Gideon had gathered 32,000 men for a battle against the Midianites. Imagine Gideon's reaction when God told him that 32,000 men were far too many. God lowered the number of men for the battle down to just 300 men. It's amazing—Gideon trusted that his coach knew better than he did. In the end, God was right, and Gideon won the battle against the Midianites.

Life Challenge

We can learn a lot from Gideon's example of trust and obedience. He listened and obeyed his coach even when, to him, it didn't make sense. We can all do the same. We can ask God to help us make good choices instead of relying on our own ideas. God is able to coach us just like He coached Gideon to victory against the Midianites!

Prayer

God, help us to do things Your way. Thank You for being our coach and teaching us to do what is right. In Jesus' name. Amen.

God Knows Your Every Thought

God knows our every thought and understands our needs better than we do.

Bible Talk

If you feel comfortable, you can ham it up for this activity and pretend to be psychic. You can even give yourself a silly name like "Sally the Magnificent." **Everyone, think of a number between 1 and 100. I'm going to try and guess what number you're thinking about. Ready?** Start pointing at children and saying random numbers. If you happen to get one right, cheer for yourself and move on. **Wow, I didn't do very well, did I? I guess this proves that I definitely can't read minds. I don't know what you're thinking.**

I may not be able to read minds, but guess who can? Allow several volunteers to answer. **God can read all of our minds. In fact, He understands every thought and feeling we have. He's our creator and knows us even better than we know ourselves. Psalm 94:11 says, "The Lord knows all human plans." That can sometimes seem uncomfortable, considering the wrong thoughts we might sometimes have. But this verse also means God understands us even when no else does! It means God knows our deepest desires, deepest hurts, and most importantly, our deepest needs.**

Conclusion

Because God knows us so well, we can always rely on Him to help us have what we really need. God knows what is best for us! What an amazing thought!

Close in prayer.

Psalm 94:11
The Lord knows all human plans.

Going the Extra Mile

Activity

Help students form pairs. **I want the older person in each pair to try and tell your partner about the best restaurant you've ever been to, but without talking. Ready? Go.** Give them about two minutes. **Now let's switch roles. This time I want the younger person in the pair to describe the most fun activity you did last summer, but again without talking.** Give them about two minutes. **Good job, everyone!**

- **How much did you understand of what your partner tried to communicate to you?**
- **What sort of frustrations did you have?**

Fortunately with God, He knows every thought we have. We are completely understood, and we don't have to be frustrated.

Bible Discussion

In the Bible, there is an interesting story of how the Israelites, God's chosen people, were unhappy about being in the wilderness after Moses had led them out of Egypt. The Israelites did not know what they were going to eat or drink, and they became worried and angry at Moses. Let's see what happens next. Have a student read Exodus 16:11–18 aloud. **God had provided food for the Israelites to eat! Even after they complained, God still gave them what they needed.**

- **Why do you think the Israelites chose to complain and not trust God?**
- **Just like the time God gave the Israelites what they needed, when might kids your age need to trust God to give them what they need?**

Life Challenge

God understands you even when no else can. When you're frustrated that friends, teachers, or parents don't understand you, you can feel good about knowing that God does! God knows what is best for you all the time. We can trust God because He knows us best!

Prayer

God, thank You that You know us inside and out. Help us to trust You to give us what we need. Thank You for understanding us when no one else can. In Jesus' name. Amen.

Leaning on God

No matter how smart or how rich we are, we always need to depend on God's wisdom.

Bible Talk

Today we're going to find out what it means to say we depend, or lean, on someone. Find a partner, stand back-to-back, and lean back against each other. Now, if you are the person whose name comes first in the alphabet, slowly move away from your partner and see if he or she can stay in the leaning position without falling over. Allow time for students to try this. Students should repeat the activity, each time increasing the distance they are leaning. Partners can take turns being the one who moves away.

How far can you lean and still stand up?

If you didn't fall over when your partner moved away, were you really leaning on him or her? Why or why not?

When you couldn't stand up after your partner moved away, it showed how much you were depending, or leaning, on him or her. When we make choices every day, we can show how much we depend, or lean, on God. Proverbs 3:5–6 says, "Trust in the Lord with all your heart and lean not on your own understanding; in all your ways submit to him, and he will make your paths straight."

Conclusion

When we lean on God's wisdom, it means that we pay attention to His Word, ask Him for help in making our choices, and put His wisdom into practice. No matter how much money we have, or how smart we are, we need God. God is always there for us to lean on!

Close in prayer.

Proverbs 3:5–6

Trust in the Lord with all your heart and lean not on your own understanding; in all your ways submit to him.

Going the Extra Mile

Activity

Let's see if we can find some information about what people today might do if they are leaning on God's wisdom. Have students form groups of three to six. Give each group several newspapers and/or news or celebrity magazines and scissors. **In your group, look through the newspapers and magazines. Cut out articles (pictures and/or written descriptions) of successful people.** After groups have cut out several articles, ask them to show and describe the articles they found.

- **What makes these people successful? Are these people successful because of their actions or appearance?**
- **Do the articles give you any clues about whether or not any of these people are depending, or leaning, on God's wisdom? How might God evaluate these people's success?**
- **If these people were trying to act in a way that showed they were leaning on God's wisdom, what might they do?**

It's not wrong to be successful in some of the ways we've read about, but whether or not a person leans on God's wisdom is the measure of true success.

Bible Discussion

Saul, the very first king of God's people, forgot to lean on God's wisdom. He made some wrong choices. Let's find out what happened next and see whom God chose to take Saul's place. Have a student read 1 Samuel 16:1–13.

- **Why do you think God cared about the kind of heart the next king would have?**
- **How can kids today show they are leaning on God's wisdom?**
- **Who do you know who leans on God's wisdom? What does that person do or say?**
- **How can you show you are leaning on God's wisdom?**

Life Challenge

Sometimes it might be hard to believe that leaning on God's wisdom is the right thing to do. Especially when people have done things we don't like, or when we're worried or afraid, we might forget to ask God for His wisdom. But every day we can remember that no matter what situation we're in, we have a loving and powerful God to lean on.

Prayer

Lord, we're so glad we can always lean on You. Thank You for giving us Your wisdom. Help us to put Your wisdom into practice. In Jesus' name. Amen.

No Eyes, No Ears

Only God knows the wonderful things He has planned for our lives.

Bible Talk

What is something you have heard of but never seen in real life? For example, I've heard that a cheetah can run faster than a car, but I've never seen it happen. Allow students time to respond with answers such as a comet, a waterfall, a submarine, a famous actor, etc.

Now, what is a sound that you've heard about but never heard in real life? For example, I've heard that the sound of a space shuttle launching into space is louder than five planes taking off at once. But I've never heard the sound of a space shuttle taking off. Allow students to respond with answers such as a lion's roar, an explosion, an avalanche, etc. **There are many things we've heard of but never experienced for ourselves.**

The Bible tells us about something else we haven't seen, heard of, or even thought of yet! First Corinthians 2:9 tells us: "What no eye has seen, what no ear has heard, and what no human mind has conceived—the things God has prepared for those who love him." As we continue to grow and learn about God's love and care for us, we don't really know what wonderful things He has planned for us in the future. We know God's plans are always good and He will teach us to love and obey Him, but we still do not know what lies ahead in our future.

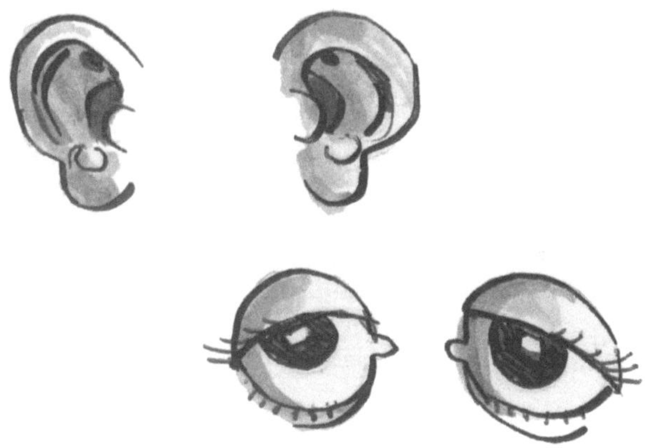

Conclusion

It's exciting to think about the special things God has planned just for you and me. His plans are the best!

Close in prayer.

1 Corinthians 2:9
What no eye has seen ... no ear has heard ... no human mind has conceived ... God has prepared for those who love him.

Going the Extra Mile

Activity

Let's create movements with our hands and arms to remember 1 Corinthians 2:9 and to remember God's wonderful plan for our lives. Say the words of the verse and demonstrate the motions below. Ask students to imitate your motions.

What no eye has seen—Cover both eyes with both hands.

What no ear has heard—Cover both ears with both hands.

And what no human mind has conceived—the things God has prepared—Take both index fingers and point to head.

For those who love him—Place both hands over heart.

If time and interest permit, students can work in pairs to create their own motions for the words of the verse.

Bible Discussion

The Bible tells us about a young man named David, who discovered that God had something special planned for him to do. Who remembers what David did? (David fought a giant named Goliath.) Have students read the following verses aloud and then answer the questions.

- **In 1 Samuel 17:4–7, how is Goliath described?**
- **In verses 8–11, what does Goliath say to challenge the Israelites?**
- **When David decided to fight Goliath, what was King Saul's response to him in verse 33?**
- **In verses 38–40, what did Saul try to make David wear? What did David take with him to fight Goliath?**
- **What was the outcome of the fight, in verses 48–50?**

No one could have imagined that God would use David to defeat Goliath. God had a plan for David to defeat Goliath and become friends with King Saul. Eventually, David became king of Israel!

Life Challenge

When we know God has a plan for us, we can trust in His plan, even when we do not know what the plan may be. Because God loves and cares for us and wants what's best for us, His plan will never fail.

Prayer

Lord, thank You for having a special plan for each of us. Teach us to trust in You and Your love for us. In Jesus' name. Amen.

A Cheerful Giver

God wants us to cheerfully give to Him.

Bible Talk

Let's pretend that we're eating squash. Pretend to eat. **Now, show me by your facial expression the way you would feel if you had to eat squash. Would you be happy, sad, angry, or excited to eat squash?** Allow a few seconds for children to show expressions. **What if you were playing basketball? Show me how you would feel if you were playing basketball right now.** Allow a few seconds for children to show expressions. As time permits, repeat with other examples (eating ice cream, taking a test at school, swimming, studying spelling words, etc.).

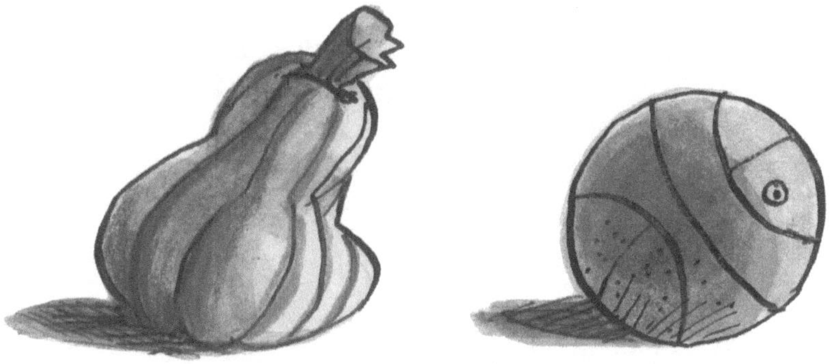

Depending on what we're doing, our attitudes can be anything from excited to nervous to happy. But no matter what we're doing, God wants us to do it cheerfully. When we give our time and money to God, we can give to Him cheerfully. Second Corinthians 9:7 says, "God loves a cheerful giver."

Conclusion

If a boy gave you a gift but he was frowning when he gave it to you, you probably would not want to open the gift. When we give to God and are happy to be able to give to Him, God is glad to receive our gifts.

Close in prayer.

2 Corinthians 9:7
God loves a cheerful giver.

Going the Extra Mile

Activity

Help students form three groups. Pass out sheets of paper and markers or crayons to each group. Assign each group a topic: money, possessions, or time. **In your groups, I'd like you to write ways you could cheerfully give to God by giving your money, time, or possessions. For example, if your group was assigned possessions, you could give the paintbrush set you received last Christmas to a class of younger children in our church. I'm sure they would have lots of fun painting as they learn about God.** Allow a few minutes to complete the task. Invite students to share ideas.

Bible Discussion

Let's read a story about a widow who cheerfully gave all she had. Have a student read Mark 12:41–44 aloud.

- **How would you describe the widow's actions?**
- **How do you think the rich people felt as they put their money in the treasury?**
- **Who did Jesus say actually gave more? In what way did she give more?**
- **Why was the poor widow's offering more pleasing to God?**

Life Challenge

It's easy to think someone who gives a lot of money to our church must be very important to God. But in God's eyes, it doesn't matter how much we give. What's most important to God is our attitude when we give to Him. We can give cheerfully and with an attitude of love—that's what really counts!

Prayer

Dear Lord, help us to have the right attitude when we give to You. Thank You for always giving us what we need. In Jesus' name. Amen.

Let Us Bow

When we worship God, we show our love and respect for Him.

Bible Talk

If I were a king or queen, what would you do to show me respect? Allow students to respond. **If I were a king or queen, you would bow or curtsy to show me respect.** Demonstrate a bow and curtsy. **Let's have everyone do a bow or curtsy.** Students can respond. **If I were a soldier in the military, what would you do to show me respect?** Allow students to respond. **If I were a soldier in the military, you would salute to show me respect.** Demonstrate a salute. **Let's have everyone salute.** Students can respond.

In the same way we can show respect and honor to a soldier and a king or queen, the Bible shows us we can give respect and love to God. The word the Bible uses for showing respect and love to God is *worship*. Psalm 95:6 says, "Come, let us bow down in worship, let us kneel before the LORD our Maker." Bowing and kneeling help us show love and respect for God's greatness.

What are some other ways that people today worship God and show love and respect to Him?

Conclusion

Believing in God and His power makes us want to worship Him. Whether we bow down or stand up straight, we can tell God how much we love Him.

Close in prayer.

Psalm 95:6

Come, let us bow down in worship, let us kneel before the LORD our Maker.

Going the Extra Mile

Activity

Let's play a game called Show Respect. I'll need everyone to stand in a circle. At my signal, you'll start walking around the circle. In this game, I will call out "God," "soldier," or "king." When I say "king," everyone will bow. Demonstrate a bow (from the waist with head down). **When I say :soldier," everyone will salute.** Demonstrate a salute. **When I say "God," everyone will kneel.** Demonstrate kneeling on one knee with head down. **The object of the game is to show respect in the correct way.** Students will stand and form a circle. Signal the students to begin walking around the circle. Begin to call out "God," "soldier," or "king." As the game continues, call out the words faster. **Excellent job! This game reminds us of the respect the one true God deserves.**

Bible Discussion

The Old Testament tells us the story of King Nebuchadnezzar. This king built a large, golden statue of himself. The king demanded that all the people bow down and worship his statue. But three followers of God would not bow down and worship the statue, because they believed in the one true God. The king was so angry, he wanted to throw these men into a fiery furnace! Let's see what happened next. Read Daniel 3:16–28 aloud.

- **Why do you think Shadrach, Meshach, and Abednego chose not to bow to the king's statue?**

- **How did God help Shadrach, Meshach, and Abednego?**

Shadrach, Meshach, and Abednego had a hard choice to make. But no matter what everyone else did, they chose to worship only God.

Life Challenge

There may be times when other people at school or in your neighborhood don't show they love and respect the one true God. When you have a choice to make about worshipping God, remember the example of these three brave friends and ask God's help to worship only Him.

Prayer

God, thank You for being so powerful. Help us to show love and respect for You. In Jesus' name. Amen.

No Substitutions

God is the only true God.

Bible Talk

What do we use our shoes for? Allow time for students to respond. **I'd like everyone to take off their shoes and put them on their hands like gloves.** Once you have your shoes on your hands, hold your hands up in the air. Allow time for students to respond. **Great! Now see if you can follow my directions.** Give the following directions, pausing after each direction for students to attempt the task. **Shake hands with someone. Scratch your head. Cover your eyes. Fold your hands.** *(Optional: Students could try to pick up an item in the room.)* **It was pretty hard to use your shoes as hands, wasn't it? It wouldn't work to substitute shoes for hands!**

In the same way shoes can never substitute for our hands, nothing can ever substitute for God. Jeremiah 10:10 says, "The Lord is the true God; he is the living God, the eternal King." Since God is the only true God, we can't substitute anything or anyone else in God's place. Some people might say there is no God or they might think other gods are real. But the Bible tells us that there is only one true God.

Conclusion

When we become a part of God's family, we are saying that we believe that only one true God exists and that we will love and obey only Him.

Close in prayer.

Jeremiah 10:10

The Lord is the true God; he is the living God, the eternal King.

Going the Extra Mile

Activity

Print the letters of the alphabet down the middle of a large sheet of paper or whiteboard. Provide several markers in a variety of colors. **Today we're going to work together to see if we can write words or phrases that describe the one true God. Each word or phrase will begin with a specific letter of the alphabet. Let's see if we can come up with a word or phrase using the letter *S*.** As time permits, lead the students to suggest words or phrases that describe God—and have them write each word beside or near the appropriate letter of the alphabet, using a variety of colored markers. If students need help thinking of words or phrases, ask questions such as:

- **What words would you use to describe God?**
- **What are some great things God has done?**
- **What does God do to keep His promises to us?**

Bible Discussion

The Bible tells us about a story in which people were worshipping a false god named Baal. God's prophet, Elijah, challenged the prophets of Baal to a contest. A wood altar was built, and the true God was supposed to send fire to burn up the altar. Let's check out the story and find out what happened. Have a student read 1 Kings 18:25–29, 36–39 aloud.

- **How did God show He was the one true God?**
- **How did the people respond to what they had seen?**

In the contest against the prophets of Baal, God proved He is the only true God. Elijah knew there are no substitutes for the power of the only true God.

Life Challenge

We may not have to choose between worshipping a false God like Baal and worshipping the one true God, but every day we can remember to show our love and praise to God. And we can help others learn about Him too.

Prayer

God, thank You for being the one true God. Help us to share with others that You are the one true God. In Jesus' name. Amen.

Showing Our Faith

Real faith in God is shown by our actions.

Bible Talk

Today we're going to practice climbing a mountain. I need everyone to stand up and follow me. Begin to demonstrate swimming motions with your arms. **Is everyone following me? Keep climbing the mountain.** Continue demonstrating swimming motions. **Finished! Climbing mountains is hard work, but were we really practicing climbing a mountain?** Allow a few responses. **What did our actions show we were really doing?** Allow a few responses. **Our actions showed that we were practicing swimming.**

We don't want to get things mixed up like that when we say we have faith in God. Our actions have to show our faith. We can't say we have faith in God but then act in ways that don't show our belief in God. That's what happened in our game. We said we were practicing to climb a mountain, but we were really doing something else. God tells us in the Bible in James 2:17, "Faith by itself, if it is not accompanied by action, is dead." That means God wants us not only to SAY we have faith in Him, but to also DO what we say we believe.

Conclusion

If we say we believe in God but don't act in ways that show our faith, it's like our faith is fake. So every day, look for ways you can act to show that your faith is the real thing!

Close in prayer.

James 2:17

Faith by itself, if it is not accompanied by action, is dead.

Going the Extra Mile

Activity

Crumple a large sheet of paper into a ball. *(Optional: Play this game with a beach ball or other soft ball.)* Have the students form a large circle. Assign each student a number. Stand in the center of the circle. **Let's play a game where we can name actions that show our faith in God. I will toss the ball in the air and call out a number. The person with the number I call must come to the center of the circle, catch the ball, and name an action that shows faith in God. For example, reading the Bible is an action that shows faith in God. Then the person who caught the ball stands in the middle of the circle, throws the ball in the air, and calls out a number for another person to catch the ball. We can play until everyone's number has been called.** Lead the game. Continue as time permits.

Bible Discussion

Let's look at a book in the Bible that has many examples of people who used actions to show real faith in God. Assign students to read the following passages aloud: Hebrews 11:1–2, 7–8, 23, 30.

- **Who are some of the people who acted to show their faith in God? What did they do?**
- **What definition of *faith* is given in these verses?**
- **How would you define *faith* in your own words?**

Everyone in these examples showed they had real faith in God—by their actions. They did not just say they believed in God; they also showed their faith in God to people around them.

Life Challenge

When we show our faith in God with our actions, it means we have real faith in God. The Bible says our faith in God without any actions is dead. Something that is dead is not able to show actions. Our faith is alive when our actions show how much we love and want to obey God. Reading God's Word, the Bible, praying to God, being obedient to God, and following His commands are all ways we can show our faith is alive.

Prayer

Father God, thank You for showing us what real faith in You means. Help us to show our faith in You by the actions we do. In Jesus' name. Amen.

What the Soul Needs

God designed us to need His love and to give our love to Him.

Bible Talk

Tell me your favorite food. Allow several volunteers to answer. **Now everyone think of your favorite food and then raise your hand. Are you thinking of it? Keep your hand up if you would like your favorite food for lunch today. Keep a hand up if you'd also like it for dinner tonight. Now, keep your hand up if you want it for breakfast tomorrow. How about lunch tomorrow?** Some children may keep a hand up no matter how long you keep the activity going. That's okay; just enjoy the laugh with them. **Some of you may think you'd like to eat your favorite food over and over and over again, but I bet you'd get sick of it eventually. God made us to enjoy a variety of foods for our health.**

But we are more than our bodies. There's an invisible part of us that thinks and feels and controls our actions. Sometimes we call that our soul. That's the part of us that feels love. We need to love and be loved. Our souls need to love God and accept His love back. Without God's love, a soul starves for what it needs to be healthy. Deuteronomy 6:5 says, "Love the Lord your God with all your heart and with all your soul and with all your strength."

What are some of the ways God has shown His love to you? (He sent Jesus. He gives me friends and family. He protects me.)

In what ways can you show how much you love God? (pray, follow His commands, sing praise songs)

Conclusion

Every day we can give our souls what they need by loving God and accepting His love in return.

Close in prayer.

Deuteronomy 6:5

Love the Lord your God with all your heart and with all your soul and with all your strength.

Going the Extra Mile

Activity

Help students form groups of three to six. Give each group paper and pencils. **People on a diet will often follow a weekly schedule of what to eat. For example, on Monday it may be grapefruit and milk for breakfast, then a salad for lunch, and so on. Your group's task today is to create a weeklong "soul diet." We know that the soul needs to give and receive love, especially God's love, in order to survive and grow. In your group, make a plan about what you would do every day of the week to give love to and receive love from God and others. Try to list at least two things you would do each day of your soul diet schedule.** Give students seven to ten minutes to complete the task. Then invite groups to share their diets. **Those are some terrific soul diets!**

Bible Discussion

The Bible talks about a diet of love in our lives too. Have a student read 1 John 4:7–12, 16 aloud. **By loving God and each other, John says, God's love will grow in us. And it is God's love that we must rely on, according to verse 16. Only God's love can nourish our souls.**

- **According to these verses, what is the best example of love?**
- **What might a kid your age do to remember God's love?**
- **When is it easy to show God's love to others? When might it be hard?**
- **What can you do when you need help showing love?**

Life Challenge

Loving God and others can be a daily priority. We can love God and love others anytime and anywhere. God is pleased when we show Him how important loving Him and others is to us. Let's start a diet of love for our souls today.

Prayer

Lord, thank You for making our whole selves—body and soul. Help us to love You and others the way You love us. In Jesus' name. Amen.

Who's Your Master?

Jesus wants us to show we love God more than we love money.

Bible Talk

I need two volunteers who really like people to notice them. Ask two volunteers to stand on opposite sides of the room. **When I give the signal, our volunteers will both start doing anything they can think of to get your attention. They might call out your name, clap their hands, or do a funny dance—just to get you to look at them. You'll get to decide who to watch. Ready? Go!** Give students 10 to 15 seconds to engage in the activity. **Thank you!** *(Optional: If time permits, allow two other volunteers to repeat the activity.)* **Our volunteers did a great job!**

How did you decide whom to watch?

What made it hard to choose whom to watch?

Was it possible to watch both at the same time? Why or why not?

It was pretty hard to watch both of our volunteers at the same time, wasn't it? There are some things in our lives we can do at the same time. For example, we can usually eat a meal and talk with a friend or family member at the same time. However, the Bible tells there are two things we CANNOT do at the same time.

In Matthew 6:24, Jesus said, "No one can serve two masters.... You cannot serve both God and money." Jesus was telling us that we can't really love God if we're loving money more. Having money isn't bad, but Jesus wants us to understand that loving God is more important than trying to get the most money.

Conclusion

Our choices about what we do and say show what we think is most important. Be thankful for the money you have, but let everyone know that you love God more than you love money!

Close in prayer.

Matthew 6:24

No one can serve two masters.... You cannot serve both God and money.

Going the Extra Mile

Activity

Give students paper and pencils. **Make a list with words or pictures of all the things that people say they love.** Give students several minutes to complete this task. Then allow volunteers to share their lists.

Thank you for those honest answers. There are always lots of things people say they love: their pets, candy bars, video games, and more. But today we've been talking about what it means to say we love God. Turn your papers over and write your ending to this sentence: "We can love God by ..." Let's see how many different endings we can write. Allow students time to write sentence endings. Then ask for volunteers to share their endings, counting how many different endings are suggested.

No matter how old or how young you are, there will be times every day when you can show how much you love God.

Bible Discussion

A very rich king who lived in Bible times wrote some proverbs, or sayings, that talk about how we can show love for God in the way we use money. Have students take turns reading aloud the following verses: Proverbs 11:25–26, 28; 14:21; 15:16; 16:16. Discuss each proverb with these questions.

- **What does this verse tell us about what is most important in life?**
- **What do you learn about how to use money to show love for God?**
- **When is a time a kid your age could follow the advice in this proverb?**

Life Challenge

Think about a time this week when you can show you love God—in your words, in your actions, and especially in how you use your money!

Prayer

Dear Lord, thank You for Your love and for the good things You give us. Help us every day to see ways in which we can give our love back to You. We choose to serve and love You. In Jesus' name. Amen.

Always Tell the Truth

God wants us to always tell the truth.

Bible Talk

I'm going to say three sentences about myself. Two of the sentences will be true, but one will be a lie. See if you can guess which sentence is the lie. Say three sentences, making it fairly easy for students to guess which sentence is the lie. After volunteers identify the lie, say, **Now I need a volunteer to stand up and tell us two true sentences about yourself and one lie about yourself. Then we'll guess which sentence is the lie.** As time permits, allow several volunteers to compete in the activity.

In this activity, you had to think about what lie you were going to say. Sometimes, however, we might lie without really thinking about it—and just hope we don't get caught.

Colossians 3:9 says, "Do not lie to each other, since you have taken off your old self with its practices." Because we love Jesus, we don't want to do things in the same old way. We want to obey God and be people who always tell the truth, even when it's hard.

Conclusion

People who lie can't be trusted. Their friends and families know they can't depend on them and can't believe what they say. That's why God wants us to always tell the truth.

Close in prayer.

Colossians 3:9

Do not lie to each other, since you have taken off your old self with its practices.

Going the Extra Mile

Activity

Let's play a game like Hot Potato. Playing this game will remind us that no one wants to get caught telling a lie. Have the students sit in a circle. If you have a large number of students, form more than one circle. Give an object (beanbag, paper cup, small ball, etc.) to a student in the circle. At your signal, students will begin passing the object around the circle. After 10 to 20 seconds, call out, **Gotcha!** The student holding the object describes a time when a kid his or her age might be tempted to tell a lie. Repeat the activity as time permits.

- **What are some reasons why kids lie?**
- **Why is it important for Christians to tell the truth?**
- **What can we do when we need help to tell the truth?**

Lying can be a real problem for kids—and adults! It's good to know that God will help us obey Him and tell the truth.

Bible Discussion

One of God's followers, named Paul, knew how much trouble telling lies could cause. Have a student read Colossians 3:7–10 aloud.

- **What are some of the things Paul said the people in God's family need to stop doing?**
- **What difference does it make to know that a friend or someone in your family can be counted on to tell the truth?**
- **How do you feel about someone you know who sometimes lies?**

Lies can cause a lot of problems! Paul reminded us that when we become Christians, it's like we are putting on a new self that tries never to lie.

Life Challenge

Lying hurts everyone involved, including the liar. The sin of lying causes others to doubt a person, even when he or she later tells the truth. Liars have a hard time building friendships, because they can't be believed. So every day, do your best to be a truth teller in every situation.

Prayer

Lord, we need Your help in reminding us to always tell the truth. Help us to tell the truth, even if it means getting ourselves in trouble. Give us the strength to be truthful. In Jesus' name. Amen.

Concentrate on Jesus

We can concentrate on Jesus and not let distractions get in the way of loving and obeying Him.

Bible Talk

Today we're going to have a staring contest. A staring contest is when two people stare into each other's eyes until one person looks away. Ask for two volunteers. For this activity, it may be better to use older kids who are more familiar with the game.

When I say "Go," stare at each other until one person looks away. Ready? Go! After volunteers stare for a few seconds, start trying to distract them by making funny faces and weird noises. Once one looks away, tell them both they did a great job and have them sit down. If they're both staring after 30 seconds or so, congratulate them both and ask them to sit down. *(Optional: Help all children form pairs and participate in a staring contest.)*

A staring contest is hard enough without a lot of distractions, isn't it? What's a distraction? Allow a few moments for answers. **That's right! Distractions are things that take our attention away from something we should be paying attention to. For example, a TV show you really like might distract you from finishing your homework. Other distractions might be sports, friends, or video games.**

There's a verse in the Bible that talks about keeping focused on Jesus—without letting anything distract you. Invite a volunteer to read Hebrews 12:2 aloud. **When we fix our eyes on Jesus, it means we choose to love and obey Him. We don't let anything distract us from doing what Jesus wants us to do.**

What are some ways we can choose to love and obey Jesus?

What might keep a kid your age from focusing on Jesus?

Conclusion

Every day we can stay focused on Jesus. We can concentrate on doing what He wants us to do. We can ask God's help so things like video games, watching TV, playing sports, and spending time with friends don't distract us from loving and obeying Jesus.

Close in prayer.

Hebrews 12:2
[Let us fix] our eyes on Jesus, the pioneer and perfecter of our faith.

Going the Extra Mile

Activity

Help students form groups of three to six. Have groups discuss the following questions, which you can write on a whiteboard or large piece of paper.

- **What types of activities are easy for a child your age to concentrate on and why?**
- **What types of activities are hard for a child your age to concentrate on and why?**
- **When is it hard for a child your age to remember to love and obey Jesus?**
- **When is it easy for a child your age to remember to love and obey Jesus?**

After about five minutes, discuss their answers with the entire group.

Bible Discussion

One of Jesus' disciples was Peter. Let's read and act out a story in the Bible, in which Peter learned what it meant to keep his eyes on Jesus. Invite two volunteers to act out the parts of Jesus and Peter. Read or ask a student to read Matthew 14:22–33. Volunteers will demonstrate the action of Peter trying to walk on water and Jesus rescuing him.

- **What made it hard for Peter to keep his eyes on Jesus?**
- **What did Peter learn about Jesus?**

Life Challenge

Concentrating on Jesus is a daily challenge. We have so many distractions like TV, friends, sports, school activities, and computers. None of these things is bad, but sometimes they keep us from remembering how important it is to do what Jesus wants. It can be easy to lose our focus, just like Peter did. We can ask for God's help to wake up every day this week ready to concentrate on Jesus all day long.

Prayer

Jesus, we want to concentrate on loving and obeying You every moment of every day—because that's the happiest way to live! In Jesus' name. Amen.

Get Strong in Obeying God

Reading and studying God's Word helps us get strong in obeying God.

Bible Talk

Today we're going to do some exercises. Let's see if everyone can do five sit-ups. Demonstrate and allow time for students to respond. Continue with the following instructions, demonstrating and pausing for students to respond after each instruction. **Now let's see if we can do a few push-ups. Show me you can do five knee bends. Let's count to ten while we jog in place. Great effort! You can take a rest and sit down now.**

If we want to have strong muscles and healthy bodies, we have to exercise on a regular basis.

What happens if we don't exercise?

Without exercise, we'll end up with out-of-shape bodies and weak muscles. Exercise helps us become strong.

Conclusion

Just like we have to exercise our bodies to become strong, we can exercise to become strong in obeying God. When we read and study God's Word, the Bible, it's like we are exercising to become strong in obeying God. In Psalm 119:28, 32 we read, "Strengthen me according to your word.... I run in the path of your commands." These verses remind us that paying attention to God's Word helps us know how to obey God's commands.

Close in prayer.

Psalm 119:28, 32
Strengthen me according to your word.... I run in the path of your commands.

Going the Extra Mile

Activity

When people start an exercise routine, they usually plan a schedule of when they are going to exercise. Tell me what an exercise schedule might look like for someone who wants to be a good baseball player. Allow time for students to suggest ideas.

Help students form groups of three to six. Give each group paper and pencils. **Today in your groups, I want you to plan a schedule of when kids your age might read and study God's Word to become strong in obeying God.** Describe to students the different times each week when you read and study God's Word. **Now, think about what things you do in a typical week and list when and where you might hear about, think about, read, study, or memorize God's Word.**

Give groups about five minutes to complete the activity. Then let groups present their work. **Those are great ideas for exercising to become strong in obeying God. Thank you!**

Bible Discussion

One of the best times God's Word helps us obey God is when we're tempted to sin—to disobey God. God's Word helps us be strong enough to obey. When Jesus lived on earth, He showed us how important God's Word is in helping us obey. Have a student read Luke 4:1–13 aloud.

- **What did Jesus say was the most important thing to do?**
- **What helped Jesus obey God when Satan wanted Him to do wrong?**
- **How can God's Word help you when you are tempted to sin?**

If we've been exercising by reading and studying God's Word, we'll be strong enough to obey when we are tempted to sin.

Life Challenge

Every day there will be times when we choose whether or not to obey God in the things we say and do. Remembering the right things God's Word says to do can help us be strong in obeying God. This week, plan a way you can exercise and get strong in obeying God.

Prayer

Lord, thank You for giving us the Bible so we can become strong in obeying You. Help us remember Your commands. In Jesus' name. Amen.

God Sees Your Every Move

God sees our every move and will help us obey Him.

Bible Talk

I'm going to give you a rare opportunity today. I'm going to turn my back, and you can all have a chance to make any kind of funny faces you want at me. Turn your back. **Ready? Go!** Give the children a few seconds to make funny faces. Then turn around. **I bet you had lots of fun making those faces at me!**

I couldn't see what you were doing, but can you tell me who COULD see? Allow several volunteers to respond. **God saw every silly face you made. In fact, God sees everything we do. In Bible times, a man named Jonah tried to run away from God. You see, Jonah was a prophet. His job was to speak for God. God asked him to give a message to the people of Nineveh. Jonah didn't want to do it, so he tried to run away. Can anyone run away from God?** Let the children answer. **Of course not! God sees every move we make. Jonah couldn't get away with trying to run from God. Who can tell how this story ended?** Let a volunteer tell or briefly summarize Jonah 1–3. **Jonah discovered that God knew everything he did. He learned to obey God, and he went to Nineveh and gave the people the message that God had asked him to tell them.**

Conclusion

We can never hide from God. He sees all that we do. Read Psalm 119:168 aloud. **The words *precepts* and *statutes* mean God's commands that we read in the Bible. This verse helps us learn that because God knows us so well, He will help us obey Him. With God's help, we can always try to do the right thing.**

Close in prayer.

Psalm 119:168

I obey your precepts and your statutes, for all my ways are known to you.

Going the Extra Mile

Activity

I need several volunteers to play a game of hide-and-seek. Invite three or four volunteers to come forward. It may be easier to play the game if the volunteer to be hidden is small. After volunteers have come forward, say, **Here's how we're going to play the game. I will choose one volunteer to be hidden. Then I'll cover my eyes and count slowly to ten while you hide this person somewhere in this room.** You may need to have an adult leader help volunteers hide the child. Slowly count to ten and then find the child. If you can't find the child, ask for hints until you find him or her. **I know you did your best to hide ______** (name of volunteer), **but surely you knew that I'd find ______** (him or her).

You hid your classmate very well. However, because I knew that ______ (name of volunteer) **was in this room somewhere, I knew I would have found ______** (him or her) **eventually. The Bible tells us God knows where we are at all times. He doesn't even have to look for us!**

Bible Discussion

The story of Jonah shows us that God sees our every move and knows everything about us.

- **What did God know about Jonah?**
- **What are some of the things God knows about us?**
- **What does God do to help us obey Him?** (answers our prayers for strength to obey Him, gives us parents and teachers at church to help us know how to obey)

Life Challenge

We can remember every day that God knows everything about us. Even when we might wish we could hide from God—because we're tempted to disobey Him—it's good to know that if we ask Him, He will help us obey Him. We can choose to love and obey God.

Prayer

Lord, You watch over everything and everyone. We know You are always with us. Help us remember that we can't run, hide, or ignore You. Help us to obey You when You ask us to. In Jesus' name. Amen.

Hasten to Obey

We can be quick to obey God's commands.

Bible Talk

Have students stand. **I'm going to say some actions. As I say each one, I want you to do that action in slow motion. Then when I give the signal, I want you to do the same action, but quickly. Here's the first action: Walk like a penguin.** Students should begin walking in slow motion like penguins. After 15 seconds, signal the students to begin moving quickly. Repeat the activity for several more actions (such as walk like a gorilla, swing from a tree like a monkey, dribble a basketball, swim, etc.). **Good job! I can see that you really know the difference between doing something slowly or quickly.**

The Bible uses the word *hasten* to mean "be quick." Psalm 119:60 says, "I will hasten and not delay to obey your commands." When God gives us a command, we can hasten, or be quick, to obey Him. If everyone did the opposite—acted slowly to obey God—we'd never learn to obey Him!

Conclusion

God wants us to be quick with obeying His commands because obeying God is one of the best ways we show our love for Him.

Close in prayer.

Psalm 119:60

I will hasten and not delay to obey your commands.

Going the Extra Mile

Activity

Let's play a game in which we hasten (be quick) to obey. Help students form two equal teams. **I am going to give you a list of things everyone on your team must hasten to do together.** Write items in the following list on paper or a whiteboard: do five jumping jacks, pat your head seven times, bend and touch your toes four times, clap hands over your head two times. **The team that finishes the list of things first will be the winners. Get set! Go!** Allow time for both teams to complete the tasks. **You all are good at hastening to obey!** Announce a winner. Encourage all students to give each other high fives for completing the tasks.

Bible Discussion

Let's find out what a man in the Bible named Abram (later called Abraham) did to hasten to obey God. Have a student read Genesis 12:1–5 aloud.

- **What command did God give to Abram?**
- **What did Abram do after God gave the command?**
- **Why might it be easy for a kid your age to hasten to obey God? Why might it be hard for a kid your age to hasten to obey God?**

Life Challenge

Abram hastened to obey God's command to leave his country, even though he was 75 years old! No matter how young or how old we are, we can hasten to obey God too. When we obey God, we show our love for Him.

Prayer

Father God, help us to hasten to obey Your commands. Thank You for loving us so much. In Jesus' name. Amen.

Jesus Says

We can always strive to imitate Jesus and not imitate evil.

Bible Talk

Let's play a game of Simon Says. For those of you who don't know how to play the game: I'll do an action like patting my head. When I say "Simon Says" and tell you to "pat your head," you do it. If I tell you to "pat your head" without saying "Simon Says" first, don't do it. If you do, you're out. Play the game for a short time. You don't need to finish the game. **Great job, everyone!**

Do you realize that every day of our lives is like a game of Simon Says? We could call this game Jesus Says. Because we want to love and obey God, we try to act in a way that is pleasing to God. Ephesians 5:1 says, "Follow God's example, therefore, as dearly loved children." What does it mean to follow someone's example? Allow several volunteers to answer. Be sure the idea of imitating gets mentioned. **We can follow God's example by imitating what Jesus would do. In our game, if you imitated me when I didn't say "Simon Says," you were out. Well, in the same way, if we imitate anything other than what Jesus would do, we are disobeying Him.**

Conclusion

Every day when you're deciding what to say and do, think about what Jesus would do—and then imitate it! We can ask for God's help to obey, and He is always ready to forgive us when we've disobeyed.

Close in prayer.

Ephesians 5:1

Follow God's example, therefore, as dearly loved children.

Going the Extra Mile

Activity

Help students form groups of three to six. **I'm going to say a situation. Then, in your group, talk about what a kid your age would do to imitate Jesus in that situation.** Read each situation from the list below. Allow groups several minutes to talk about possible responses. Then ask one or more groups to tell their ideas.

Situations:

Your little sister is having trouble tying her shoes. What would Jesus do?

Your friend asks you to let him copy your homework. What would Jesus do?

You found a $10 bill on the floor. Later, your mom asks if you have seen some money she lost. What would Jesus do?

Your big brother is hurrying to finish his chores so that he can get to his job. What would Jesus do?

Great work! Sometimes we might think about imitating people we hear about in the news, or we might want to imitate our friends. The best person to imitate is Jesus!

Bible Discussion

In the Bible we read about a man who thought others should imitate him. Have a student read 1 Corinthians 4:14–17 aloud. **Paul's boldness in asking people to imitate him is amazing. In this letter to the Christians who lived in the city of Corinth, he asks them to imitate him because he taught them to know and love Jesus. Paul had the right to ask people to follow his example.**

- **What do you know about Paul?**
- **What did he do to help others come to know the good news about Jesus?**

Paul was one of our greatest Christian leaders, and he spread the good news of Jesus throughout the world. He was jailed, beaten, shipwrecked, and eventually killed for following Jesus. We can read many of Paul's letters in the New Testament.

Life Challenge

Think about your words and actions. Would you want people to imitate them? Why or why not? If we love Jesus, we can live a life that's an example of Jesus' life to others. We can ask for God's help so we can say to others, just like Paul, "Imitate me." Think about what changes you can make to be an imitator of Jesus so you're a good example for others. Because whether we like it or not, others are imitating us. Younger children in the church are looking up to you and want to be just like you.

Prayer

Lord Jesus, help us to imitate You. Help us be a good example to others just as Paul was. In Jesus' name. Amen.

Listening When God Calls

We can always be ready to listen to what God is saying to us—and be ready to obey when He calls us to action.

Bible Talk

Show me what you would do to make sure you couldn't hear what I'm saying. What would you do to block out my voice so you couldn't hear me? Students will probably cover their ears or make loud noises. Affirm their demonstrations. **What do we miss out on when we don't listen?** Let a few volunteers respond.

In the Bible there is a great story about a boy named Samuel who lived in the tabernacle with a priest named Eli. *(Optional: Ask a student to read 1 Samuel 3:2–10 aloud.)* **After Samuel had gone to bed one night, God called out, "Samuel! Samuel!" Samuel went to Eli, thinking it was he who had called, but Eli sent him back to bed. After Samuel got back in bed, God called him again. Samuel went to Eli again, and Eli sent him back to bed. Then it happened again! This time Eli realized it was God calling Samuel and told him to listen very carefully to what God had to say. The Bible says in 1 Samuel 3:10 that when God called him again, Samuel said, "Speak, for your servant is listening." As it turned out, God had big plans for Samuel to do important work for Him.**

Conclusion

We can be like Samuel and listen to God, because He has something to tell us every day. We can hear God talking to us when we read His words in the Bible. We can hear His voice when we listen to Bible stories or when our parents and teachers at church tell us about God and how to follow Him. Maybe God is telling you to be extra nice to someone, or to give one of your toys away to another child in need. Or maybe God just wants to say, "I love you." Let's follow Samuel's example and listen to God every day.

Close in prayer.

1 Samuel 3:10

Then Samuel said, "Speak, for your servant is listening."

Going the Extra Mile

Activity

I want everyone to stay completely silent for one full minute and listen. Try to remember everything you hear. Keep time and make sure no one makes a sound.

- **Tell me about some of the sounds you could hear while you were silent.**
- **What helped you hear those sounds?**
- **How might kids your age be able to listen to what God is saying to them?** (reading the Bible, listening to Bible stories)
- **What might keep a kid your age from paying attention to what God says?** (forgetting to read the Bible, not paying attention to Bible stories)

Bible Discussion

We've already looked at the story of Samuel and how he listened to what God had to say. Let's find out what Samuel was able to do for the Lord because he listened. Have a student read 1 Samuel 3:19–20 aloud. **God had some very important work for Samuel to do. The book of 1 Samuel tells us Samuel spoke on behalf of God to the Israelites and became their leader. He even anointed Saul as the first king of Israel. Samuel also had the courage to rebuke King Saul when he disobeyed God. Just think of how different things would have been if Samuel had not listened to God.**

- **When are some times you can listen to what God is telling you in the Bible?**

Life Challenge

God has so many important things for you to do in this world, just like He had important things for Samuel to do. It pleases God when we hear and obey Him, just as Samuel did. We can take time to listen to God every day.

Prayer

Invite the children to pray silently to God, asking for His help in listening to Him. Allow 10 to 15 seconds of silence. Then pray, **God, we pray for listening ears so we can hear what You want us to do every day. Thank You for giving us Your Word and parents and teachers so that we can learn how to love and obey You. In Jesus' name. Amen.**

Obey Today

We can love God and obey His commands.

Bible Talk

I want each of you to stand up and pat your head. Remember that no matter what other commands I give you, patting your head is the most important thing to keep doing. After you say the following commands, pause briefly after each one to allow time for the children to obey. **Now, rub your tummy. March in place. Bob your head. Stop! That was really hard, wasn't it? The more commands that I gave, the harder it was to concentrate on the first and most important command to pat your head.**

Deuteronomy 28:14 says, "Do not turn aside from any of the commands I give you today." Every day God wants us to remember that His commands are the most important thing. That way, when our day gets busy and we have lots of other things to do, we won't forget to love God and follow His commands.

Conclusion

Playing soccer, going to school, and playing with our friends are some of the fun things we might do. But no matter what we're doing, we can always show our love for God and obey Him.

Close in prayer.

Deuteronomy 28:14
Do not turn aside from any of the commands I give you today.

Going the Extra Mile

Activity

Help students form groups of three to six, and give them paper and pencils. **In your groups, I would like you to write down at least five things a kid your age might do in a typical day. Start from the time a child gets up in the morning and end with going to bed.** Give students five minutes to complete the task. Invite several groups to share their ideas. **Very good. Now, talk with your group again and list ways to obey God's command to do good to all people** (see Galatians 6:10) **while doing the activities you listed.** Give students a few minutes. Invite several groups to share their ideas. **It's great to know that even with our busy lives, God is always with us and will help us to obey His commands.**

Bible Discussion

Have a student read Deuteronomy 28:12–14 aloud.

- **What do you learn about God when you read these verses?**
- **What do you learn about how God wants us to act?**

Life Challenge

Think of a way you can remember to show your love for God and obey His commands during the things you do every day. You can memorize a Bible verse or make a verse poster for your room. And don't forget God's promise to bless you—to show His love for you!

Prayer

Lord, we want to show others our love for You. Help us to obey Your commands every day. In Jesus' name. Amen.

Obeying Mom and Dad

God wants us to obey our parents so we can learn good ways to live.

Bible Talk

I'm going to give you a list of tasks your mom or dad may sometimes ask you to do at home. As I call out each task, if you don't like to do the task, stand up and silently act it out. If you like to do the task, stay seated. Call out each of the following tasks one at a time, pausing after each one to allow time for the students to respond.

Go to sleep in your bed.

Make your bed.

Pick up your toys.

Eat breakfast.

Do your homework.

Turn off the TV.

Thank you. You may sit down now. Sometimes we think it would be so great if we didn't have to obey other people. But even grown-ups have people they need to obey.

Obeying everything your parents tell you to do may not be easy. But God gives you parents so that when you obey them, you learn good ways to live. Ephesians 6:1 says, "Children, obey your parents in the Lord, for this is right." The Bible tells us it is right to obey our parents.

Conclusion

Moms and dads can teach us many things, especially when we're young. When we learn to obey moms and dads, it helps us learn to obey other people like teachers and coaches. Even better, obeying moms and dads helps us learn to obey God!

Close in prayer.

Ephesians 6:1

Children, obey your parents in the Lord, for this is right.

Going the Extra Mile

Activity

Pass out sheets of paper and markers or crayons. **I would like you each to draw a line down the middle of your paper. Then on one side of the line, draw a picture of a way that it is easy for you to obey your mom or dad. On the other side of the line, draw a way that is hard for you to obey. Your pictures can show you making your bed or washing dishes or any other ways your mom or dad asks you to obey.** Allow a few minutes for students to complete the activity. Invite a few volunteers to show their drawings and tell what they will do to obey their mom or dad this week. **God knows when it's hard for you to obey, and He promises to help you do what's right.**

Bible Discussion

The Bible tells us more about what parents and children can do. Have a student read Ephesians 6:1–3 aloud.

- **What do you think it means to honor your parents?**
- **What promise do you read in these verses?**
- **What might kids your age do to honor their parents?**
- **Is it hard or easy to honor and obey parents? Why?**

Life Challenge

We might not like to think about how important it is to obey people like our parents, who are teaching us what it means to live in good ways. But God's Word reminds us how great it can be to have people who care about us and who want to help us learn right actions.

Prayer

Dear Lord, thank You for giving us moms and dads. Show us how to obey our moms and dads every day. In Jesus' name. Amen.

Right and Wrong

As followers of God, we can stop doing wrong actions and start doing right actions.

Bible Talk

Black and white. Hot and cold. What kind of a comparison am I making? Allow time for students to respond. I was naming words that are the opposite of one another. When two things are opposite, it means they are very different from one another. What are some other opposites you can think of? Allow time for students to respond. If needed, call out each of these words one at a time, pausing for students to name the opposites: salt, fast, short, happy, light, quiet, stop, dead, sunny, full, boy. *(Optional: Secretly whisper opposites, such as salt and pepper, to students, assigning each word to a different student. At your signal, students should begin walking around the room and saying their assigned words aloud, trying to find who has the opposite words.)*

The Bible tells us about opposites too. Listen for the opposites in these verses. Ephesians 4:31–32 says, "Get rid of all bitterness, rage and anger, brawling and slander, along with every form of malice. Be kind and compassionate to one another, forgiving each other, just as in Christ God forgave you."

What words did you hear that are opposite of each other?

Verse 31 uses words like *bitterness*, *rage*, *anger*, *brawling*, *slander*, and *malice* to describe wrong actions. Verse 32 uses words like *kind*, *compassionate*, and *forgiving* to describe right actions. The Bible gives us these examples of opposites so we can know which actions are wrong and which actions are right.

Conclusion

God wants us to put aside, or stop, any wrong actions and instead do what's opposite—start doing right actions.

Close in prayer.

Ephesians 4:31–32

Get rid of all bitterness, rage and anger.... Be kind and compassionate to one another, forgiving each other.

Going the Extra Mile

Activity

I will need three volunteers for this activity. Have three volunteers come to the front of the room. **I will give each volunteer a word to act out. See if you can guess what the word is and then call out the opposite of the word that you guessed.** Assign words to volunteers, referring to the list on the previous page.

Good job! You were able to guess the words and their opposites because of the volunteer's actions. Now let's see if you can think of some right or wrong actions that show whether or not we are following God. For example, if you are taking a test at school and you see a way to cheat by looking at a friend's answers, what is the wrong action that should stop? What is the right action to do? Allow time for students to respond and then to suggest other situations and actions. **Our right or wrong actions show whether or not we are following God. God will help us choose right actions.**

Bible Discussion

The Bible tells us about a man who thought it was VERY important to know which wrong actions to stop doing and which right actions to start doing. Listen to find out what he did. Have a student read 1 Kings 3:5–13.

- **What did Solomon ask God for? Why?**
- **What could he have asked God for instead?**
- **When might a kid your age need to ask God for help in knowing what's right and what's wrong?**

Solomon knew he would need God's help to be a good king. Choosing between right and wrong isn't always easy. It's good to know God will answer our prayers too when we ask Him for help to make good choices.

Life Challenge

We see all kinds of opposites every day—like salt and pepper. The Bible tells us about some very important opposites: things that are right and things that are wrong. If we are doing what is wrong, we can stop and with God's help do the opposite—we can do what is right!

Prayer

God, thank You for showing us what's wrong and what's right. Help us every day to choose to do right. In Jesus' name. Amen.

Run with Perseverance

Following Jesus every day takes perseverance.

Bible Talk

I'd like everyone to stand up. We are going to see how long we can do something that's easy at first, but gets harder and harder the longer we do it. Let's see how long we can run in place. Have students run in place at any pace they wish. Continue for several minutes or until some students seem to tire. **Now let's see how long we can hold our arms up in the air.** Allow several minutes for children to hold their arms up. *(Optional: Lead students in one or more additional exercises, such as jumping jacks, hopping on one foot, etc.)* **Thank you! You may sit now. In order to keep doing something hard, it takes perseverance.**

Who can tell me what someone is like who has perseverance?

Someone who has perseverance is not willing to give up. But running and holding our arms up in the air aren't the only things that take a lot of perseverance. Being a follower of Jesus takes perseverance too. Hebrews 12:1 says, "Let us run with perseverance the race marked out for us." Being a follower of Jesus (doing what He wants) is like running a long race. The goal of the race is for followers of Jesus to love and obey Him for as long as they live.

Conclusion

Sometimes it's easy to give up being obedient to Jesus. But God will help us persevere and follow Jesus—we can run and not give up!

Close in prayer.

Hebrews 12:1

Let us run with perseverance the race marked out for us.

Going the Extra Mile

Activity

Help students form two groups. Have the groups stand on opposite sides of the room. Give each student a sheet of paper and pencil. **Each of you should write on your paper a way in which a kid your age can follow Jesus.** What can kids do to show that they love and obey Jesus? (read the Bible, go to church, obey Bible commands, pray) Allow time for the students to write answers. **Now each of you fold your paper to make a paper airplane.** Allow time for students to complete the task. Give help as needed. **Now, when I give the signal, fly your airplanes across the room to the other group. When you catch an airplane, open it up and read the way to follow Jesus. On the other side of the paper, write or draw a picture of a time when you can do what is written on the paper.** Lead students to complete the activity. *(Optional: As time permits, students can make and fly additional paper airplanes.)*

Bible Discussion

Long ago in Bible times, there was a man who didn't give up doing what he knew God wanted him to do, even when it was hard. This man's name was Daniel. We often hear about Daniel's bravery when he was put in the lions' den. But let's find out what it was that Daniel persevered in doing. Have a student read Daniel 6:6–11 aloud.

- **What did Daniel do every day? How many times did he do it?**
- **Why do you think Daniel kept on praying, even when he knew it was against the king's new law?**
- **What are some things kids your age can often do to show they are persevering in following Jesus?**

Not just in this story, but in all the stories of Daniel's life, we read that he showed his love and obedience to God.

Life Challenge

Every day we make choices that show whether or not we are persevering in following Jesus. We might choose to tell the truth, be patient with a younger brother or sister, or stand up for a friend. All these choices and many more show that we are not giving up in loving and obeying Jesus.

Prayer

Dear God, we want to obey You every day. Help us to follow You with perseverance and not to give up loving You. In Jesus' name. Amen.

Standing Alone with Jesus

Following Jesus takes courage.

Bible Talk

Everyone, let's get ready to clap in unison (that's all together)! Start clapping on the count of three. One ... two ... three! Lead the children to clap in unison for about ten seconds. **Great job! Now let's do it again, but this time I also need one person to stand over to the side and shout "Yee Haw! Yee Haw!" while doing a funny dance. Who would like to volunteer?** Avoid letting groups of children volunteer. The volunteer needs to act alone. **Now we're ready to try it with our volunteer shouting and doing a funny dance all alone. Is everyone ready to clap in unison? One ... two ... three!** Lead the children to clap in unison for about ten seconds while the volunteer does a funny dance. Then tell the volunteer, **Good job! Thank you for being funny all by yourself.**

How hard was it to clap in unison with your friends?

How hard do you think it was for our volunteer to do something all alone?

It can be hard to stand up all alone and be different, because everyone is looking at you.

Sometimes following Jesus feels just like doing something completely different from what everyone else is doing. God tells us it takes courage to follow Him. Read Joshua 1:7 aloud.

Conclusion

God knows how hard it can be to love and obey Him. The next time you obey God by being friendly to the kid no one else likes, by reading your Bible, or praying before your meal, remember God is proud of you for having the courage to do the right thing.

Close in prayer.

Joshua 1:7

Be strong and very courageous. Be careful to obey all the law.

Going the Extra Mile

Activity

Help students form groups of three to six, and give them paper and pencils. **In your groups, I would like you to write or draw three situations in which a kid your age would need to show courage.** Allow groups time to complete the task. **One group at a time, let's look at each situation and rank them on a scale of one to ten, with one being the situation that requires little or no courage and ten being the situation that requires the most courage.** Allow groups time to share their situations, and then lead them in ranking the situations.

Bible Discussion

Jesus knew better than anyone what it meant to stand alone. In fact, He endured the ultimate in standing alone. Have a student read Matthew 27:35–44 aloud. **Jesus took on humiliation, death, and the sins of the world all by Himself.**

- **What did people say to make fun of Jesus?**
- **Why was Jesus willing to show courage and do the right thing?**

Life Challenge

Remembering the courage Jesus showed when He died on the cross helps us to know that He can help us have the courage to do what's right too. Yes, you may get laughed at and made fun of, but Jesus will stand with you.

Prayer

Thank You, Jesus, for standing alone and dying on the cross to save us from our sins. Help us to have the courage to stand alone for You. We know that You will be there with us and give us strength. In Jesus' name. Amen.

The Earth Is the Lord's

God wants us to take care of His world.

Bible Talk

Who has ever thumb wrestled before? If children are unfamiliar with thumb wrestling, demonstrate with a partner how to thumb wrestle. **Thumb wrestling is when you hold someone's hand and try to pin down each other's thumbs. The only rule is that you must hold on to each other's hand the entire time during the game. The first person in each pair to pin down the partner's thumb gets to stand up and tell something that God has made in the world. I need everyone to find a partner.** If you have an odd number of kids, participate in the game yourself. **Is everyone ready to thumb wrestle? Go!** Play several rounds of the game.

Psalm 24:1 says, "The earth is the Lord's, and everything in it, the world, and all who live in it." Everything that we see in this world belongs to God. He created the land, the plants, the animals and even us—we belong to God too.

Conclusion

Because God created everything we have, He wants us to take care of what He has given to us.

Close in prayer.

Psalm 24:1

The earth is the Lord's, and everything in it, the world, and all who live in it.

Going the Extra Mile

Activity

Help students form groups of three to six. Write the words of Psalm 24:1 on a whiteboard or large sheet of paper for everyone to see. **In your groups, I would like you to use your hands to create motions for the Bible verse. Psalm 24:1 says, "The earth is the LORD's, and everything in it, the world, and all who live in it." Practice the motions so that you can show them to all of us.** Allow five to ten minutes for groups to complete the task. Invite groups to demonstrate their motions to the larger group. **Outstanding! This verse reminds us that God wants us to care for His world and everything that is in His world.**

- **Because the earth belongs to God, what are some ways we can care for the earth?**
- **Because people belong to God, what are some ways we can care for people?**

Bible Discussion

You'll need seven small groups or seven pairs (or just seven individuals, if your class is small). Give each group Bibles. **God created the world and everything in it in only seven days! I will give each of your groups a few Bible verses to read. Once you are finished, we will discuss what God made on each of the seven days.** Assign one of these passages to each group:

- Genesis 1:3–5
- Genesis 1:6–8
- Genesis 1:9–13
- Genesis 1:14–19
- Genesis 1:20–23
- Genesis 1:24–31
- Genesis 2:1–3

Allow ten minutes for the groups to read.

- **Based on your Bible verses, what did God create on the first day? Second day? Third day? Fourth day? Fifth day? Sixth day? Seventh day?**
- **What do we learn about God from these verses?**

Life Challenge

God wants us to care for everything in His world. Every day we can do something to show God we appreciate what He has given to us. We can do things like pick up trash from the ground at school, help our neighborhood stay clean, and be kind to our families—the people God made.

Prayer

God, thank You for creating the world for us. Show us ways to care for Your world. In Jesus' name. Amen.

Turn Away

When we sin, we can ask for God's forgiveness and turn away from our wrong actions.

Bible Talk

Today we'll play a game called Turn Away. I'll need everyone to stand and line up shoulder to shoulder. Have all students line up on one side of an open area in the room. Stand on the other side of the room. **I will call out several directions. For example, when I say "walk," everyone walks toward me. When I say "freeze," everyone stops and freezes. When I say "turn," everyone turns around and walks in the other direction. When the first student reaches me, that student will become the caller and we'll play a new round. Let's play!** Lead students in the game. Switching commands rapdily will make things more interesting. *(Optional: include variations like "crawl," "hop," etc.)* Play the game as time permits.

In our game, when I said "turn," you had to turn and walk in the opposite direction. In order to show we love and obey God, sometimes we have to turn away from doing something that is wrong. The Bible tells us in Psalm 119:59, "I have considered my ways and have turned my steps to your statutes." This verse shows us that when we realize we have sinned, we can turn away from our wrong actions and ask God for forgiveness to help us do what is right.

Conclusion

Turning around and walking away from something that is not right is not always easy. But that is just what God wants us to do—and He'll always be ready to help us!

Close in prayer.

Psalm 119:59

I have considered my ways and have turned my steps to your statutes.

Going the Extra Mile

Activity

Pass out sheets of paper and markers or crayons to each student. **We're going to draw road signs. Road signs are signs you may see while you're riding in a car. What are some road signs you've seen before?** Allow volunteers to answer. Allow up to 15 minutes for students to draw signs. Invite the students to show their signs.

- **Which of these road signs do you think are the most important to follow? Why?**
- **Which of the signs that we've seen help us to know what to do when we have done wrong actions?**

Bible Discussion

The Bible tells us about a king who had to decide whether or not he was going to turn away from doing wrong. Let's find out what he did. When Josiah was king, he led the people in cleaning up the temple. One of the people working in the temple found a book. This book was the Book of the Law—God's commands in the first five books of the Old Testament. When the king read the words in the book, he was so upset that he tore his robes (2 Kings 22:11)**! He realized that he and God's people had been disobeying God in an important way. Listen to what he did next.** Have a student read 2 Kings 23:1–3 aloud.

- **What did Josiah and God's people promise to do?**
- **Why do you think Josiah wanted the people of Judah to turn away from their wrong actions?**
- **When is a time a kid your age might need to turn away from doing wrong?**

Life Challenge

We can turn our wrong actions into right actions. We can remember that when we sin, all we need to do is ask for God's forgiveness and for His help to do the right thing. Let's thank God for His forgiveness and help when we do wrong things.

Prayer

God, thank You for Your forgiveness and help when we sin. Help us to turn away from our wrong actions and do what is right. In Jesus' name. Amen.

Weird for God

Sometimes being a follower of God means doing what seems odd in order to do the right thing.

Bible Talk

On the count of three, I want everyone to do something weird. You can make a funny face, get up and dance, whatever you want—as long as you stop when I say so and don't hurt anyone around you. Ready? One, two, three! While children are moving, pick a few children and comment positively on what they're doing. (Example: I like that crazy face you're making!)

Stop! Wow, that was some weird stuff. Did you know God asks those of us who follow Him to do things that are right in God's eyes but may seem odd to other people? That's what happened to a man in the Bible.

What have you heard about a man in the Bible named Naaman? Allow a few moments for answers. **Naaman was a powerful commander in the army of the king of Aram, but he had a problem. He had a terrible disease called leprosy. Leprosy does awful things to your skin. Naaman asked the Lord's prophet Elisha how he could be healed of his leprosy. Second Kings 5:10 says that Elisha told Naaman, "Go, wash yourself seven times in the Jordan, and your flesh will be restored and you will be cleansed." Naaman thought it was the weirdest thing he had ever heard. Here he was with a skin disease, and God wanted him to get in a nasty river … and not just once but seven times! Well, Naaman became angry about it, but he did it anyway. After the seventh dip into the Jordan, he was healed by God!**

Conclusion

Naaman did what God wanted him to do even when it seemed weird to him. God may want you to do something others think is odd or weird. Maybe God will ask you to be a friend to someone no one else likes. Maybe God will ask you to take the money you saved up and give it to a poor family. Maybe God will ask you to become a pastor! Just remember that even when obeying God seems odd to others, we can trust that God knows what's best for us. Read Acts 5:29 aloud.

Close in prayer.

Acts 5:29
We must obey God rather than human beings!

Going the Extra Mile

Activity

Sometimes it's fun to think about doing weird things. Listen to each of these situations. Then tell what weird thing you might do in that situation. Read the situations below one at a time. Give several students a chance to respond. Be sure to laugh along with the students' weird answers, as long as they are not hurtful. For example, a student may decide to spend $1,000 on bubble gum.

Situation 1: A stranger gives you $1,000 cash to use however you want.

Situation 2: You can design your bedroom any way you want.

Situation 3: Your mom says you have to do something besides watch TV.

Situation 4: Your teacher at school tells you to draw a picture of anything you want.

Situation 5: You have three friends over to play. What do you do together?

Bible Discussion

We had a good time thinking of weird things to do. In the story of Naaman, God told Naaman to do something that sounded weird: wash in a dirty river seven times.

- **What do you think Naaman thought when he first heard what God wanted him to do?**
- **Why do you think Naaman decided to do what God said?**
- **What do you think Naaman learned about God?**

When Naaman didn't want to do what God said, his servants encouraged him to obey God. Naaman must have been very glad that his servants helped him. Have a student read aloud 2 Kings 5:10–15.

Life Challenge

All of us—the people who love and obey God—can help each other obey God too. We can remind each other of the instructions in God's Word, and we can pray for each other.

Prayer

Lord Jesus, help us to obey You. Help us to rely on each other to do the right thing too. Thank You for the chance to obey You even when it is hard. In Jesus' name. Amen.

What's between You and Jesus?

When anything keeps us from following Jesus, God can help us remove the obstacle.

Bible Talk

Ask for a volunteer to stand behind the other children, who will be seated. Hold up three fingers. __________ (name of volunteer), **how many fingers am I holding up?** Volunteer answers. **Was it easy or hard to see my fingers? Now I want everyone to stand up and hold your hands in the air to block __________'s** (name of volunteer) **view.** Hold up six fingers now. **__________** (name of volunteer), **how many fingers am I holding up?** The volunteer answers. **Was it easy or hard to see my fingers this time? Why?**

It's easy to see something when there are no obstacles in the way. When you all stood up and became obstacles, __________ (name of volunteer) **had a hard time seeing my fingers. Following what Jesus wants us to do works the same way. When we are clearly focused on Jesus, we can see what Jesus wants us to do. However, when we let obstacles get in the way, it's much harder to love and obey Jesus.**

A rich man once came to Jesus and asked him how to get to heaven. Jesus told him to sell all his possessions and follow Him. The man's possessions were obstacles keeping the man from following Jesus. So Jesus told the man to get those obstacles out of the way. We can have obstacles that keep us from following Jesus too. Maybe we're so focused on spending time with friends or playing video games or watching TV that we forget about doing important things that God wants us to do. Friends, video games, and TV aren't bad, but they can become like obstacles to loving and obeying Jesus.

Conclusion

Think about what might be your obstacle to following Jesus. Ask for God's help in removing the obstacle so you can see Jesus and follow Him.

Close in prayer.

Matthew 19:21

"Go, sell your possessions and give to the poor, and you will have treasure in heaven. Then come, follow me."

Going the Extra Mile

Activity

Give each child a disposable cup and a marker. **On your cup, write a word that reminds you of something that might keep you from paying attention to Jesus and following Him.** (Examples: computers, sports, money, TV, video games, friends, etc.) It's okay for a word to be written more than once. After students have written on their cups, invite several volunteers to help you arrange the cups in a bowling-pin pattern. **Each of these cups represents an obstacle that might come between you and Jesus so you can't see how to follow Him. These things aren't wrong to have or to enjoy, unless they become more important than loving Jesus and obeying Him.**

Let's see if we can knock down all the obstacles. Have the students line up several feet from the cups. Give the first student in line a ball. That student rolls the ball, trying to knock over as many obstacles as possibe. Continue with additional students as time permits, resetting cups as needed. **We did it! We knocked over all the obstacles that might keep us from following Jesus.**

Bible Discussion

Let's take a closer look at the story of the rich man. Have a student read Matthew 19:16–26 aloud.

- **What choice did the rich man make? Why do you think he made this choice?**
- **What are some choices kids your age could make to show they want to follow Jesus?**
- **What can you do when you need help in following Jesus?**

Every day we can show by our choices that we want to follow Jesus.

Life Challenge

Always be on the lookout for any obstacles that may keep you from following God. When we find one, we can ask God's help to get rid of it right away. Nothing is more important than showing how much we love God.

Prayer

Lord, give us the wisdom to see when an obstacle keeps us from following You. Then give us the strength to love and obey You. In Jesus' name. Amen.

Celebrate!

We can celebrate God's great actions and His goodness.

Bible Talk

What are some things we celebrate? Allow students to respond. **I am going to give you two sentences to finish. I would like you to tell me how you celebrate.**

My favorite thing to do at Christmas is ...

On my birthday, I like to ...

Allow students to respond, and tell your sentence completions too. **We celebrate lots of things for different reasons, and each of our families likes to celebrate things in different ways. Celebrations are times of joy and happiness. When we celebrate something, it normally means that we are happy about something or for someone.**

The Bible tells us something we can celebrate about God. Psalm 145:4, 7 says, "One generation commends your works to another; they tell of your mighty acts.... They celebrate your abundant goodness and joyfully sing of your righteousness."

What do you learn about God from these verses?

What do these verses say we can do to celebrate?

Conclusion

Just like we look forward to birthday or Christmas celebrations, we can look forward to celebrating God's great actions and goodness. We can celebrate by singing songs of praise like we do here at church and by praying. So get ready to celebrate!

Close in prayer.

Psalm 145:4
One generation commends your works to another; they tell of your mighty acts.

Going the Extra Mile

Activity

Give each student a sheet of paper, a pencil, and markers. **Today we're going to make a book of celebration about God's great actions and goodness to us. On your sheet of paper, draw a picture or write a story about something great God has done, or some way in which He has shown goodness to you or your family. Use the markers to decorate the page.** Allow time for students to complete the task. To help students think of what to write or draw, ask, **What is something awesome that God has made? What amazing action have you read in the Bible that God has done? What good thing has God helped you have?** The student who finishes first may make a cover for the book, adding a title and decorating it. When all students have completed their papers, collect the papers and staple together with the cover. Briefly flip through the book, showing the pictures and reading the stories.

Bible Discussion

In the New Testament, Jesus told a story about a father and two sons. The father gave one son a lot of money, but the son left home and spent it all! When he ran out of money, he decided to go back home. Let's find out what happened and who celebrated. Have a student read Luke 15:20–24.

- **How did the father act when he saw his son?**
- **What did the father do for his son?**

God is like the father in the story. He loves us so much and is willing to forgive us when we do wrong things. And when we come back and ask for forgiveness, like the younger son did, God is excited and celebrates because we did the right thing. The son celebrated too because he was so glad for his father's love and forgiveness.

Life Challenge

No one wants to miss out on a party or celebration. So every day, remember that God has invited you to celebrate His great actions and goodness.

Prayer

Dear God, it's exciting to hear about all the great things You have done. We love You and are so thankful for Your goodness to us. In Jesus' name. Amen.

Clap Your Hands

We can praise God in many ways.

Bible Talk

Do a short clap pattern to get students' attention. Clap three times quickly, pause, and then repeat three quick claps. **With a partner, I'd like you to create your own clap patterns. You can make a short clap pattern or a long clap pattern or a combination of both.** Allow time for students to form pairs and create and practice clap patterns. Invite pairs to demonstrate their clap patterns. **Thank you! Those were some great claps!**

What are some of the reasons people clap their hands? Allow time for students to give answers. **We can clap our hands to show support for someone, like when someone gets an award. We can clap our hands to music as a way to recognize beats. The Bible talks about clapping hands too. Psalm 47:1 says, "Clap your hands, all you nations; shout to God with cries of joy." Clapping hands is a way we can praise God. When we clap our hands for God, we show honor and respect to Him.**

Conclusion

There are many ways we can show praise to God. We can sing songs, write prayers, and play music. We can simply clap our hands to show praise to God.

Close in prayer.

Psalm 47:1

Clap your hands, all you nations; shout to God with cries of joy.

Going the Extra Mile

Activity

Have students form pairs or trios. Pass out Bibles to each group, or write the words of Psalm 47:1 on a whiteboard or large sheet of paper. **With your partners, create a rhythmic way to say Psalm 47:1. You can clap your hands or snap your fingers or even tap your feet.** Demonstrate saying the verse in a rhythmic pattern. Allow time for students to create and practice rhythmic patterns. Invite groups to demonstrate ways of saying the verse. **Making rhythms like these is a way of making music! You all did an excellent job of praising God!**

Bible Discussion

The Bible tells us about King David and a time when he praised God. Let's find out what he did. Have a student read 2 Samuel 6:12–15 aloud.

- **What did David do to praise God?**
- **What do you think it means to praise God with all your might?**
- **What are some ways you have seen people in our church praise God?**

David wrote many psalms that tell of his praise and love for God. Reading David's psalms can help us praise God too.

Life Challenge

Sometimes we might think we can only praise God when we're at church. But we can praise God no matter where we are. This week, at the end of every day before you go to sleep at night, think of something that you can praise God for.

Prayer

Dear God, help us to remember we can praise You in many different ways. Thank You for giving us so many good things. We love You. In Jesus' name. Amen.

Great God

We can praise God because of His greatness.

Bible Talk

How many words can you think of that mean the same as the word *great*? Allow students to respond. (Possible answers: wonderful, awesome, cool, amazing, incredible, etc.) **There are many words that mean the same as *great*. Thanks for all your great suggestions!**

The Bible often uses the word *great* to describe God.

What are some of the reasons the Bible describes God as great?

Our God is great because He is the ruler of the world! He made the world and everything in it. He is the King of everything and there is no other God besides our God! Now that's a great God!

Psalm 95:3 says, "The Lord is the great God, the great King above all gods." Let's say this verse together. Notice where it says "great." Then we'll repeat the verse, substituting the words we thought of that mean the same as the word *great*. Lead the students in repeating Psalm 95:3 as written and then using the synonyms.

Conclusion

We can praise God for all the great things He is and the great things He does!

Close in prayer.

Psalm 95:3
The Lord is the great God, the great King above all gods.

Going the Extra Mile

Activity

Attach two posters to the wall at one end of the room. At the other end of the room, have students line up in two teams for a relay race. Give the first person on each team a marker. **We'll have a relay race. Each of you should think of a reason why God is great. When I say "Go," the first student on each team will run to your team's poster, write your reason, run back to the team, and hand the marker to the next person. Ready, go!** Allow time for students to complete the relay. Read the reasons aloud after the relay is finished.

Bible Discussion

We've been talking about the many reasons why God is so great. Now let's look at the ways we can praise God because of His greatness. Have a student read Psalm 150 aloud.

- **What do you learn from these verses about praising God?**
- **What kinds of musical instruments do we still use today to praise God?**
- **What are the ways you praise God?**

Life Challenge

Sometimes we only think about singing or praying praise to God when we're at church. But we can praise our great God no matter where we are! Let's praise God for His greatness right now.

Prayer

God, You're an awesome, great, and cool God! There's no other God greater than You. We love You because You're great. In Jesus' name. Amen.

Great Is the Lord

Nothing compares to God's greatness.

Bible Talk

I am going to give you a list of things to rate. I would like for you to show me how great you think these things are by holding up your fingers. On a scale of one to ten, hold up one finger if what I say is not great at all. Hold up to ten fingers if what I say is really great! Ready? Say the following items one at a time, pausing to allow students to rate each item: doing math problems, going to Disneyland, playing soccer, doing science experiments, watching TV, feeding the dog. If desired, add other items for students to rate, such as movies, TV shows, singers, actors, etc.

We think a lot of things are great, but the Bible tells us about someone who is greater than all the things we rated as ten. Psalm 145:3 says, "Great is the LORD and most worthy of praise; his greatness no one can fathom." God is greater than we could ever imagine! He created our world and everything in it! Nothing can compare to God's greatness.

Conclusion

Whenever you see something or hear about something that is really great, remember God's greatness. His power, His love, and His goodness all rate the highest!

Close in prayer.

Psalm 145:3

Great is the LORD and most worthy of praise; his greatness no one can fathom.

Going the Extra Mile

Activity

Divide the students into several groups. Give each group a sheet of paper and a pencil. **We're going to write prayers that give thanks and praise to God for the ways in which He shows His greatness. To begin the prayer, in your group, think of a way to complete this sentence: "I'm so glad You made …" Write the sentence at the top of your paper.** Allow time for students to complete the task.

Now trade your paper with another group and think of a way to complete this sentence: "I praise You for …" Allow time for students to complete the task.

Now trade your papers one more time and finish the prayer by completing this sentence: "God, You are so …" After students have finished their prayers, collect the papers and read the prayers aloud, or invite the groups to read the prayers.

Bible Discussion

The Bible gives us many different reasons why God is great. Let's see if we can find some of these reasons. Have a student read Psalm 145:3, 8–9 aloud.

- **What words are used to describe God?**
- **What actions of God are described?**
- **What can the people who know about God's greatness do?**

It's amazing to realize that this great God cares so much about each of us. We can give Him some great praise!

Life Challenge

It may be hard to imagine how great God really is! But as we see the ways in which God cares for us every day, and the ways He answers our prayers and helps us know what to do, we begin to see His greatness.

Prayer

God, You are so great! Thank You for all the ways You provide for us and care for us. In Jesus' name. Amen.

If You Breathe, Praise the Lord

We can praise the Lord with everything we do and say.

Bible Talk

Have you ever heard of a holding-your-breath contest? If not, you're about to witness one right now. Ask for two volunteers to stand up and face each other. *(Optional: Have all children participate in the contest.)* On your count of three, have them take a deep breath and hold it. See how long they can hold it before they have to take a breath again. Congratulate them on a job well done. **Wow, that was exciting! Did you notice that no matter how long our volunteers held out, they both had to breathe at some point? In fact, we all have to breathe. If we're not breathing, then we aren't living. Let's see what the Bible says about breathing.** Open your Bible to Psalm 150:6 and read the Scripture. **We all breathe, so we can all praise the Lord.**

What do you think it means to praise the Lord?

Those are all great answers. Praising the Lord can be done here in our church, but that's not the only place. We can praise the Lord at home, at school, while we're walking down the street, while we're playing soccer, and even while we're cleaning our rooms.

Conclusion

Remember that praising the Lord isn't just something you do on Sunday morning; it's a way of life. We don't just do it once a week—we live it! So let's get to it! Let's praise the Lord!

Close in prayer.

Psalm 150:6
Let everything that has breath praise the Lord.

Going the Extra Mile

Activity

Help students form groups of three to six. **I want your group to come up with a list of at least five things children your age might do every day. Then discuss in your groups how those things can be done in a way that praises God.** Give students five to seven minutes to complete the task. When they're finished, ask a volunteer from each group to present their list.

Bible Discussion

Some situations may be so tough that praising God seems to be out of the question. We're going to look in the Bible at just that sort of situation. I think you'll be surprised at how the people in this story praised God in very hard times. Ask a student to read Acts 16:22–25 aloud. **Isn't it amazing that even under such horrible and sad conditions, Paul and Silas could find the strength to sing praises to God?**

- **If you were in their situation, how do you think you'd act?**
- **When might praising God seem impossible?** (when I'm in trouble at school, when I'm sick)
- **When have you been in a tough time and you forgot to praise God or you didn't feel like praising God?**

Life Challenge

Praising God in tough situations can be really hard sometimes. Maybe we're sad or hurt and don't want to praise God. Or maybe we're just so busy, we don't make time. We can make an effort with every breath we take and in everything we do to give praise to God. When we praise God, it helps us to remember the love and strength of God's presence. We remember God is in control and wants what is best for us.

Prayer

God, we give praise to You today for giving us this time together. We thank You for what we've learned about praising You in all things. Help us to remember every day to praise You no matter what happens. In Jesus' name. Amen.

Remember the Lord's Goodness

We can remember God's goodness to us.

Bible Talk

What is a really good time you remember having on a vacation trip or at a birthday party? What is something fun you did with a friend or with your family? Allow a few students to share stories. *(Optional: Tell about a good time you've had with the students in your group.)* **What are the things you do to remember something good?** Allow students to respond. **When people want to remember good times, they often take pictures of what happened. I would like everyone to stand up and make a pose that reminds you of a good time you've had. Pretend you are posing for a picture that will be in a photo album.** Allow a few minutes for students to pose. Comment on the poses you see, and as time permits, have students tell about the good times they are remembering.

It's fun to remember the good times we've had. The Bible tells us about something God wants us to remember. Psalm 77:11 says, "I will remember the deeds of the Lord; yes, I will remember your miracles of long ago." This verse tells us to remember the good things that God has done for us—and for the people whose stories we read about in the Bible. Remembering His goodness helps us realize God is always with us.

Conclusion

There might be some days when we don't feel like anything good is happening to us. On those days especially, it can help us to remember the ways God has shown His goodness to us in the past. We can know that God's goodness never ends!

Close in prayer.

Psalm 77:11

I will remember the deeds of the Lord; yes, I will remember your miracles of long ago.

Going the Extra Mile

Activity

Pass out sheets of paper and markers or crayons. **Symbols are pictures with no words.** Give examples of different symbols such as road signs, no-smoking signs, restaurant or clothing logos, etc. **Today we're going to make symbols to help us remember the good times God gives us. Think of something God has helped you have and enjoy. It might be a family member, a pet, or an answered prayer. It might be a special friend or a fun trip or event. Now draw a symbol that will help you remember that good thing.** *(Optional: Provide play dough for the students to make sculptures as reminders of God's goodness.)* Allow time for the students to draw symbols. Invite volunteers to show and describe their symbols.

Bible Discussion

In the Old Testament we can read about many ways in which God showed His goodness to His people. One time, God told His people to make a special reminder of His goodness. Let's find out what the reminder was and what God wanted His people to remember. Have a student read Joshua 4:1–7.

- **What did God's people do as a reminder of God's goodness?**

- **What event did God want His people to remember?**

God knew His people would face some difficult times in the promised land, so He wanted them to have this special reminder of His love and goodness. When we face difficult times, it's good for us to have reminders of God's goodness too.

Life Challenge

This week be on the lookout for the ways in which God shows His goodness to you. Even if you don't have a stone (like the Israelites had), or another symbol to look at as a reminder of God's goodness, you can always remember what He has done and thank Him for His love.

Prayer

Father God, thank You for Your goodness to us. Help us to remember the ways You help us and provide for us. We are so glad that You love us. In Jesus' name. Amen.

Sing Praises to God

We can all sing praises to God all the time.

Bible Talk

Let's all sing together "Jesus Loves Me." You can substitute any simple praise chorus or hymn. If you don't feel comfortable leading the song, arrange to have a choir member or a worship leader lead the song. **That was beautiful! If you think you're a good singer, raise your hand. If you don't think you're a good singer, raise your hand.**

We may all wish that we were good singers, but when it comes to praising God with songs, it really doesn't matter whether you're a good singer or not! In fact, Psalm 47:6 says, "Sing praises to God, sing praises; sing praises to our King, sing praises." Notice how the verse doesn't say "sing praises only if you're a good singer." Everyone can participate in singing praises to God.

Conclusion

God loves to hear us sing praises to Him. And when we're singing His praises, it reminds us of all the good things He does for us.

Close in prayer.

Psalm 47:6

Sing praises to God, sing praises; sing praises to our King, sing praises.

Going the Extra Mile

Activity

Help children form groups of three to six. Mix older and younger children together, as well as stronger and weaker singers together, if possible. **The Bible tells us to sing praises to God. We don't have to do that by only singing what we already know. We can use new music to sing praises to God. In your groups, finish this song with your own words:**

We love to praise You.
You are a great God because …

Finish that verse and create another verse if you want for us to sing for God. Be ready to teach your song to the rest of us. Give students five to seven minutes to work. Then have the groups present their songs. Congratulate everyone on a job well done. **Thanks so much for those terrific songs. Singing praises to God and even creating new songs to sing, like you just did, are great ways to show your love for God.**

Bible Discussion

Psalm 47 shows just how wonderful and exciting it is to sing praises to God. Have a student read Psalm 47 aloud.

- **What are some of the reasons this psalm gives for praising God?**
- **Why is it good to sing praises to God with other members of His family?**

The author sure knew just how important it was to sing praises to God. When God's family sings praises together, each person helps make the praise a special time of worship.

Life Challenge

We can sing praises to God to anytime. It doesn't matter if we're at home, at school, or at church. God is always ready to hear us sing praises to Him!

Prayer

Lord, we want to sing praises to You because You are King over all the world. Help us to be ready to praise You with a song and express our love for You. In Jesus' name. Amen.

Just Ask

We can pray every day to ask God for His help to obey Him and follow His commands.

Bible Talk

Do any of you think you can take off your shoes and socks just by using your feet? Choose a student to attempt the task. *(Optional: Get a volunteer ahead of time, or if possible, invite all students wearing shoes and socks to attempt this task.)* **Ready? Go!** Narrate the actions while the student attempts the task.

Whether or not the student succeeds, say, ______ (name of volunteer) **did a great job, huh? It probably would have been quicker and easier to use hands to remove the shoes and socks. But I asked ______** (name of volunteer) **to do it the hard way.**

When we think about obeying God and following His commands every day, sometimes we try to do that task the hard way too. We try and try to obey—but we forget to first ask God for His help. Psalm 121:1–2 says, "I lift up my eyes to the mountains—where does my help come from? My help comes from the Lord, the Maker of heaven and earth." To obey God and follow His commands, we don't just have to rely on our own strength. We have help from the powerful God who created the world!

Conclusion

Anytime you need help to obey God, just ask!

Close in prayer.

Psalm 121:2

My help comes from the Lord, the Maker of heaven and earth.

Going the Extra Mile

Activity

On separate sheets of construction paper, print the following sentence starters: "It's easy to obey God when …"; "Kids think it's hard to follow God when …"; "I can pray to God and ask for His help to obey when …" Place the papers and markers around the room. Help students form groups of three to six. **In your groups, think of ways to finish each of these sentences. Have one person in your group write down your group's idea for a sentence completion. Write at least one sentence completion on each paper.** Allow five to seven minutes for groups to complete the task. Then read the sentence completions aloud.

Bible Discussion

In the book of Psalms, we can read a prayer that someone in Bible times wrote, asking God for help to obey. Have a student read Psalm 119:33–35 aloud.

- **How does the writer of this prayer describe obeying God?**
- **What things did the writer say he wanted to do?**
- **How might a kid your age say this prayer in his or her own words?**

Asking God for help to obey is something that everyone can do at any time. God loves us and is always ready to help us.

Life Challenge

Think about a time you need God's help to follow Him. Remember that God promises to help, and He also promises to love and forgive us, even when we do wrong things. Just ask!

Prayer

God, thank You so much for being ready to help us in whatever we need. We want to pray to You every day and ask for Your help. In Jesus' name. Amen.

Prayer Matters

We can always pray for people who need help.

Bible Talk

We all know the Bible tells us to pray for others. Think of someone you could pray for, but don't say the name aloud. Find a partner and use your finger to write the name of the person on your partner's back. You may write the name more than once. Allow time for children to form pairs and take turns writing names on backs. *(Optional: The children can simply write the first letter of the person's name.)*

If the person you pray for is someone in your family or a friend, raise your hand. Allow time for children to respond. **If the person for whom you pray is someone who lives in our city, raise your hand.** Allow time for children to respond.

It's great to pray for the people we see every day or every week. But there are also people we can pray for whom we NEVER see. For example, you might hear about hungry children who live far away in Africa or a family that doesn't have a home to live in. When we hear about sad situations like these, we want to help in some way. Even if we don't have what is needed to make their situations better, one way we can always help is to pray for them. That's why the Bible says in 1 Thessalonians 5:17, "Pray continually."

Conclusion

We can pray as often as we'd like to every day for people who are in need!

Close in prayer.

1 Thessalonians 5:17
Pray continually.

Going the Extra Mile

Activity

Help students form groups of three to six. Divide Matthew 6:9–13 into sections, one section for each group. Assign a section to each group. **In your group, read your section of this prayer and think of some situations when kids your age might pray each section.** Give each group paper and pencils and allow time for groups to work. Then invite each group to tell the situations they listed. *(Optional: Have groups write their own versions of their assigned sections of the Scripture.)* End the activity by asking students to say the Lord's Prayer together.

Bible Discussion

Jesus knew prayer was so important, He taught His disciples a prayer. This prayer has become one of the most famous prayers in the Bible. It's called the Lord's Prayer. Christians all over the world often pray this prayer together. Have a student read Matthew 6:9–13 aloud.

- **What are some things Jesus prays about in this prayer?**
- **Why might it be good to pray at the beginning of each day? At the end of each day?**
- **When are some times you already pray regularly? When could you start a new habit of praying?**

Life Challenge

Sometimes we are so busy, we forget to pray to God. However, God wants us to pray to Him all the time. We can pray about anything! When something wonderful happens to you, thank God. When you have a hard challenge coming up at school or on a sports team, ask God for strength. When you are sad about something, tell God how you feel and ask Him to comfort you. Try your best this week to pray about every situation you're in, and then look for the ways that God answers your prayers.

Prayer

Lord, thank You for listening to our prayers. Thank You for answering our prayers in ways that are best for us. In Jesus' name. Amen.

Watch Out!

When we pray, we can look forward to God's answers to our prayers.

Bible Talk

What do you think it means to be watchful? Allow students to respond. **To be watchful means to pay attention to what's happening around you. Let's play a game in which we practice being watchful.**

Help the students form a large circle. Stand in the middle of the circle. **I will be the leader and start an action that I want you to follow. While we're doing the action, I will choose someone to come to the center of the circle to be the next leader. I will choose this person by giving him or her a signal without saying anything. The new leader can change the action of the group and then choose another leader by giving someone his or her own signal without speaking. Let's begin.** Do an action that students can follow, like clapping or snapping fingers. Then give a signal to a new leader. Continue the activity as time and interest permit. **Good job! You had to be very watchful in order to find out who the new leader was going to be.**

The Bible tells us about being watchful too. Colossians 4:2 says, "Devote yourselves to prayer, being watchful and thankful." This verse tells us to pray often and to be watchful when we pray.

What do you think it means to be watchful when we pray?

We devote ourselves to prayer by praying often, even when we don't feel like it. Then we can watch out for God's answers to our prayers, and we can thank Him for the answers He gives us.

Conclusion

God wants us to pray often so we can know and trust Him. So every day, remember to pray and remember to watch for God's answers.

Close in prayer.

Colossians 4:2
Devote yourselves to prayer, being watchful and thankful.

Going the Extra Mile

Activity

Let's play a game to help us think about things we can pray about, and we need to be watchful at the same time. Give each student a large self-stick note and pencil. The students should write on the notes something they might pray about. Collect all notes and place each on the back of the student who wrote it. **Each of you has your note placed on your back. At my signal, you will all try to grab notes from each other. You may not hold onto or touch your own note in defense, but watch out for anyone who is trying to grab your note. If your note is grabbed, you must surrender any other notes you have collected and then sit down until the game is over.** Lead the students in playing the game until time is up or until most students are out of the game. Ask volunteers to read the notes aloud. **It's good to know God promises to hear and answer our prayers.**

Bible Discussion

Let's find out what happened when Jesus and three of His disciples prayed together. Have a student read Matthew 26:36–41 aloud.

- **What did Jesus pray about?**
- **What were Jesus' instructions to His disciples?**
- **What did Jesus find the disciples doing when He returned from praying?**

This story helps us learn that in addition to watching out for God's answers when we pray, it's important to pray about and watch for ways to obey God.

Life Challenge

We all have different prayer habits. Some of us pray with our families, and some of us may only pray when we come to church. But God is always ready to hear our prayers. Talking to God every day will help you get to know Him and follow Him.

Prayer

Thank You, God, for hearing our prayers. Help us to be watchful for the answers You give us. In Jesus' name. Amen.

A New Creation

When we become members of God's family, we live and act in new ways.

Bible Talk

Think about the toys, games, and other things you have. Allow time for students to think. **Now find a partner and each of you answer the following questions.** *(Optional: Ask and answer the questions in the large group.)*

What's the newest thing you have?

What is the oldest thing you have?

There's usually a big difference between something that is brand-new and something that is old. The Bible tells us that when we become members of God's family, we begin to live and act in new ways. Second Corinthians 5:17 says, "If anyone is in Christ, the new creation has come: The old has gone, the new is here!" Because God helps us to live and act in new ways that show our love for God, it's like we are brand-new creations.

Conclusion

As members of God's family, God gives us many new and good things. Let's thank Him!

Close in prayer.

2 Corinthians 5:17
If anyone is in Christ, the new creation has come: The old has gone, the new is here!

Going the Extra Mile

Activity

One creature that gets a new start is the caterpillar. Once a caterpillar forms a cocoon, it stays there until it develops into a butterfly. When it comes out of the cocoon, the caterpillar makes a new start as a butterfly. Pass out sheets of paper and markers or crayons. Have students fold their papers in half. **Today we'll draw a caterpillar and the beautiful butterfly the caterpillar becomes. On one half of the paper, draw a caterpillar; and on the other half of the paper, draw a butterfly. On the half of the paper with the butterfly drawing, I'd like you to write the words of 2 Corinthians 5:17.** Allow time for students to complete their drawings. **Our drawings can remind us of the new ways we can live when we believe in Jesus and become followers of God.**

Bible Discussion

When Jesus lived on earth, He taught a man named Nicodemus how to be a follower of God. Nicodemus believed Jesus was God's Son, but he asked Jesus some very important questions about what it means to be a part of God's family. Let's see what Nicodemus asked and what Jesus answered. Have a student read John 3:1–8 aloud.

- **What did Nicodemus ask?**
- **When Jesus said that Nicodemus must be born again, what do you think He meant?**

Jesus wanted Nicodemus to know that when a person becomes a member of God's family, God gives the person a new start. When a baby is born, the baby is a new creation starting life for the first time. When we believe in Jesus, we begin our lives as Christians. We start to love and obey God for the first time.

Life Challenge

Think about the things you do and say that show you are a member of God's family. All these words and actions show that you are a new creation. Every day ask God's help to show your new life as His follower.

Prayer

Dear God, thank You for helping us to live and act in new ways for You. Thank You for letting us become a part of Your family. In Jesus' name. Amen.

Excited about Heaven

We can be excited about heaven.

Bible Talk

I'll need one volunteer for this game. Choose one volunteer and send him or her to another room or area. **We're going to hide a pretend treasure in the room while our friend is in another room.** Hide a penny or some similar pretend treasure. Allow the volunteer to enter the room. ______ (name of volunteer), **this is what will happen. You are going to look for a pretend treasure somewhere in the room. If you are getting close to where the treasure is hidden, everyone will say "hot." If you are not close to where the treasure is hidden, everyone will say "cold." Ready? Go!** Allow a few minutes to play the game. Whether the volunteer does or does not find the treasure, congratulate him or her on a job well done.

In this game, we hid pretend treasures.

When you think of treasures, what kinds of things do you think of? (money, jewels, gold coins)

The Bible tells us there is a different kind of treasure in heaven. Matthew 6:20 says, "Store up for yourselves treasures in heaven, where moths and vermin do not destroy, and where thieves do not break in and steal." This verse means we can start collecting and adding to the treasures God has waiting for us in heaven. We can add to our treasures by saying and doing things that are valuable to God. When we say kind words to others, help others in need, and tell others about Jesus, we are saying and doing things that are valuable to God.

Conclusion

There are many things we don't know about heaven. But we do know Jesus is there and we are collecting treasures that can't be destroyed or stolen. It's exciting!

Close in prayer.

Matthew 6:20

Store up for yourselves treasures in heaven, where ... thieves do not break in and steal.

Going the Extra Mile

Activity

Provide paper and markers. **When have you been to a party? We're going to make party invitations to the celebration we will all enjoy in heaven. This great celebration will last forever—like a nonstop party. When we get to heaven, not only will we have our treasures to enjoy, but we will get to praise and thank God for His love for us! Anyone who is a follower of Jesus is invited.** Allow ten minutes for kids to make party invitations. Invite a few volunteers to show their invitations.

Bible Discussion

Let's find out more about our treasures in heaven. Have a student read Matthew 6:19–21 aloud.

- **What does Jesus say can happen to treasures on earth?**
- **What does Jesus say about treasures in heaven?**

Jesus wants us to be excited about heaven. Heaven will be a place where all believers and followers of Jesus will meet Him and get to live with Him forever.

Life Challenge

We can enjoy what we have here on earth, but heaven will be a better place—like no other place we've seen before. We can start storing up our treasures in heaven right now. Let's all get excited about going to heaven!

Prayer

Lord, thank You for making heaven for us. Help us to store up many treasures in heaven. Help us to tell others about heaven. In Jesus' name. Amen.

Getting to Know God

Because Jesus came to live on earth, we can know what God is like.

Bible Talk

I need a volunteer to go the other end of the room. Pick a student and have him or her stand at the farthest end of the room. **Let's all wave at** _____ (name of student). Allow time for students to respond. **Let's all say, "Hi,** _____ (name of student). **How are you?"** Students can respond.

If we had never met _____ (name of student) **before, how well would we be able to get to know** _____ (him or her) **from way over here?**

What would have to happen for us to get to know _____ (name of student) **better?**

It's pretty hard to get to know someone if you can't see the person and talk to the person. We need to be near someone in order to get to know him or her. That's why God came near to us by sending His Son, Jesus, to live on earth. God sent Jesus so that all people could get to know what God is like.

John 1:14 says, "The Word became flesh and made his dwelling among us." ***Word*** **is another name for Jesus. This verse talks about the time when Jesus was born on earth. The people who lived when Jesus was alive on earth saw the things Jesus did and heard the things that Jesus said. Some of these people wrote all about Jesus so we could get to know God. We can read about Jesus' life on earth by reading in the books of Matthew, Mark, Luke, and John.**

Conclusion

Sometimes we might feel like God is so far off that we can't really get to know Him. When we feel that way, it's good to remember that learning about Jesus is one way for us to get to know God.

Close in prayer.

John 1:14
The Word became flesh and made his dwelling among us.

Going the Extra Mile

Activity

Getting to know someone is important if you want to be that person's friend. Find a partner. If possible, encourage students to pair off with others whom they don't know very well. **Talk to your partner to find out three facts about each other. For example, you might find out your partner's middle name, favorite game, or newest pet.** Give partners several minutes to talk. Then allow volunteers to report on what they learned about their partners.

In order for us to love and follow God, it's important for us to get to know Him, just like you get to know a friend. Reading God's Word and finding out about Jesus' life on earth are great ways to get to know God.

Bible Discussion

One of the stories Jesus told in the book of Luke is a great example of how Jesus helps us learn what God is like. Listen to the story Jesus told. Have a student read Luke 15:11–24 aloud.

- **How do the actions of the father in this story help us know what God is like?**
- **How would you describe God after hearing this story?**

Jesus' actions and teachings make a big difference in helping us get to know what God is like.

Life Challenge

God wants you to get to know Him. It's amazing to think that the Creator of the world cares about getting to know each of us. Look for ways this week that you can find out more about what He is like.

Prayer

Dear God, we want to get to know You better every day. Thank You for sending Jesus so that we can learn more about You and Your love for us. In Jesus' name. Amen.

Jesus' Sacrifice

We can praise Jesus because His love for us is so great, He died on the cross for us.

Bible Talk

Listen to the words I say, and if I name something you love a lot, spread your hands out like this. Demonstrate the action. **If the item is something you love just a little, hold your hands very close together like this.** Demonstrate the action. **If it's something you love halfway between a lot and a little, spread your hands apart just a short distance. Are you ready?** Name some or all of these items, pausing after each word to let children make the actions: ice cream, broccoli, skateboarding, pizza, homework, basketball. Modify the list to reflect the likes and dislikes of your students. **I can tell that there are some things you REALLY love!**

In the Bible we read about someone who loves us much more than we love things like ice cream and pizza. Jesus loves us so much, He died on a cross to save us from our sins. Do you think He wanted to do it? Absolutely not! The night before Jesus was crucified, He prayed to His Father in heaven asking, "Father, if you are willing, take this cup from me; yet not my will, but yours be done" (Luke 22:42). **The cup Jesus talks about in this verse is His death on a cross. He didn't want to die on the cross. But because of His great love for us, He sacrificed His life and died for every one of us!**

Conclusion

It's hard to imagine someone would willingly die for another person. But that's just what Jesus did. Even on days when we feel like no one really cares about us, we can remember Jesus' great love for each one of us and praise Him for His sacrifice.

Close in prayer.

1 John 3:16
This is how we know what love is: Jesus Christ laid down his life for us.

Going the Extra Mile

Activity

Today we're going to create prayers of praise. We'll see if we can make a border of prayers that goes all the way around our room. Modify the goal according to your facility. **Our prayers will praise Jesus for His love and the good things He does for us to show His love.** Students should form groups of three to six. Give each group several sheets of paper and markers. Allow time for groups to write prayers of praise on individual papers. When the prayers are completed, attach them to the wall in a row, trying to see how long a row of prayers can be created. After all papers have been displayed, have volunteers read the prayers aloud. **When we think about the way in which Jesus has shown His love for us, we're glad to praise Him!**

Bible Discussion

One of Jesus' disciples, John, wrote some of Jesus' words when He talked about love. Let's find out what Jesus said. Have a student read John 15:9–13.

- **Why did Jesus say He was teaching about His love and His commands?** (so we would have joy)
- **What did Jesus say was the greatest way He showed His love?**
- **What can a kid your age do to share Jesus' love with others?**

Jesus loves each of us so much, He wants each of us to experience His love—and then share it with others. Jesus didn't have to die on the cross, but He chose to show His love in this amazing way.

Life Challenge

Knowing that Jesus loves each of us so much helps us be ready to share His love with others. We can make friends with kids who are hard to be friends with. We can give away some of our toys to the needy. We can stay behind and help clean up when we'd rather run off and play. When we show love for others even in little ways like that, we come closer to understanding the great love of Jesus.

Prayer

Lord, we praise You for loving us so much that You died on the cross for us even when You didn't have to. We ask Your help so that we can be ready to share Your love too. In Jesus' name. Amen.

Living Forever

If we believe Jesus is God's Son and He took the punishment for our sins, we will live forever with God.

Bible Talk

I need everyone to stand up. I want each of you to hold up one leg and hold it out in front of you in the air while I count to ten. Ready? Go! Count to ten. **Good job!** As time permits, invite volunteers to see how long they can stand on one leg. **Raise your hand if you think you could have held your leg up in the air for one minute. Now keep your hand raised if you could hold up your leg for ten minutes. How about an hour? How about ... forever?**

Of course, you can't hold your leg up forever. But there's one thing we can do forever: live with Jesus in heaven. John 3:16 says, "God so loved the world that he gave his one and only Son, that whoever believes in him shall not perish but have eternal life." This verse means God will give us new life that will last forever if we believe in His Son, Jesus.

Conclusion

What a great feeling to know that each person in the world can believe in Jesus to get the gift of eternal life!

Close in prayer.

John 3:16
God so loved the world that he gave his one and only Son, that whoever believes in him shall not perish.

Going the Extra Mile

Activity

Have students form groups of three to six. **With the people in your group, think of a slogan that describes what we receive by believing in Jesus as God's Son. Your slogan can tell about receiving forgiveness for sins, eternal life, or God's everlasting love.** Allow time for groups to work, and then have each group tell their slogans. **Now think of some motions you can do while saying your slogan.** Students can create and practice the motions before showing them to the rest of the group.

Bible Discussion

Let's look at a time in the Bible when Jesus talked to a woman about living forever with Him. Have a student read John 4:4–15 aloud. **The Samaritan woman was looked down on and disliked by other groups of people. And because she was a woman, she was considered nothing more than property. Jewish men were not supposed to talk to Samaritan women, but despite that, Jesus went to her and started a conversation. Jesus' actions were surprising!**

- **What kind of water did the woman want Jesus to give her?**
- **What do you think Jesus meant when He told the woman He would give her "living water"?** (The living water Jesus could give was eternal life—life as a member of God's family now and forever.)

Because Jesus talked to this woman, many people from the nearby town came to see Jesus—and believed in Him.

Life Challenge

We can have great joy in knowing that one day we will be living with Jesus forever in heaven. Nothing in our world lasts forever, but let's rejoice that Jesus' love lasts forever!

Prayer

Lord, thank You for giving us eternal life. Show us how to help others find eternal life with Jesus. In Jesus' name. Amen.

The One Way to Heaven

The only way we can go to heaven is through Jesus Christ.

Bible Talk

Think about your home. Think about all the windows and doors you have in your house. Guess or count quickly and tell me how many ways you could get into your house. Allow time for students to think and then respond. **Some of you live in a home with many entrances. And some of you may live in a home with just a few ways to get in. But probably all of us have more than one way to get inside, even if it's just a window.**

Let's see what the Bible says about how many ways there are to get into heaven. Jesus tells us in John 14:6, "I am the way and the truth and the life. No one comes to the Father except through me." Jesus makes it very clear in this verse that only one way to heaven exists. We go to heaven by believing Jesus is God's Son. Only because of His death can our sins be forgiven. We can't get there by being nice or making good grades or being talented at something like singing or soccer.

Conclusion

Believing in Jesus with all your heart gets you into heaven. There is no other way.

Close in prayer.

John 14:6

Jesus answered, "I am the way and the truth and the life. No one comes to the Father except through me."

Going the Extra Mile

Activity

Today we are going to create our very own mazes. Each of you will get a sheet of paper and a pencil. Draw a maze with only one entrance and one exit. But in between you can have as many dead ends as you like. Give students five to ten minutes to complete their mazes. **Now exchange your maze with someone else. Use your pencil to find your way through the maze from entrance to exit.** Give students a few minutes to solve the mazes. **Raise your hand if you made it through a maze. Good job!**

All mazes have an entrance and an exit, but there are lots of dead ends too. It's important to avoid getting stuck in the dead ends. When people think that something other than believing in Jesus will help them get to heaven, it's like they are stuck in a dead end. Working on these mazes reminds us there is only one way to get to heaven.

- **What are some things that kids your age might think will help them get to heaven?** (going to church every week, always telling the truth, being nice to everyone)

Bible Discussion

Let's look at what Jesus said about heaven and the way to get there. Have a student read John 14:1–7 aloud.

- **How did Jesus describe heaven?**

- **What do these verses help you learn about Jesus?**

- **How would you say John 14:6 in your own words?**

Life Challenge

Just like finding our way through a maze, we can follow Jesus to find our way to heaven. Without Jesus as our guide, we would be lost. We can have faith in Jesus, allowing Him to show us the way home to heaven. He IS the way!

Prayer

Lord Jesus, show us the way home to heaven. Help us to have enough faith to follow You. Thank You for guiding us. Amen.

We Win!

Because of Jesus, we have victory over sin and death.

Bible Talk

What does it mean to be a champion?

Champions are confident they will succeed at anything they do. Champions expect to win and not lose. People notice champions by the way they walk. How do champions walk? Allow several volunteers to answer. **Champions walk with their chins up, chests out, and shoulders back.** Demonstrate how a champion walks. **Let's practice walking around the room like champions.** Give students a few minutes to walk around the room. **You all look like champions to me!**

The Bible tells us God sent His Son, Jesus, to give everyone who believes in Him the chance to be a champion. First Corinthians 15:57 says, "Thanks be to God! He gives us the victory through our Lord Jesus Christ." Because of Jesus, we are champions and have victory over sin and death.

What did Jesus do to make it possible for us to have victory over sin and death? (He died on the cross to take the punishment for our sins—and is alive today.)

God promises to help us say no to sin. And as members of God's family, we will live forever with Him in heaven.

Conclusion

Every day we can walk like champions because we know that Jesus has given us victory over sin and death.

Close in prayer.

1 Corinthians 15:57
Thanks be to God! He gives us the victory through our Lord Jesus Christ.

Going the Extra Mile

Activity

Give each student a sheet of paper and a pencil or marker. **I would like each of you to draw a picture of a trophy or medal that you think all champions for Jesus should have. You can even draw yourself in the picture wearing the medal or holding the trophy.** Give students 10 to 15 minutes to complete the task. Invite a few students to share their pictures with the group. **I think every champion for Jesus should have those medals and trophies.**

Bible Discussion

Let's see what the Bible says about the victory we receive once we become champions for Jesus. Have a student read 1 John 5:3–5 aloud.

- **Based on these verses, how do we show our love for God?**
- **Who do these verses say has victory by overcoming the world?**

If we believe Jesus is the Son of God and He died on the cross for our sins, we can have victory over sin and death. That means we have God's help in choosing to do the right things. Best of all, we can live with Jesus forever in heaven.

Life Challenge

It seems like everyone wants to win at everything. Soccer teams want to win games, movie stars want to win awards, and all kinds of people want to win money! Of course, we know that everyone can't be a champion at everything. But if we trust and beieve in Jesus, we have victory in the most important ways. We win! Let's thank Jesus for giving us victory!

Prayer

Jesus, thank You for dying on the cross for our sins. Thank You for giving us victory over sin and death. In Jesus' name. Amen.

Celebrating Mom

We can thank God for mothers and others who show God's love to us.

Bible Talk

Today is the day we talk about moms, aunts, grandmothers, and other people in our lives who show God's love to us. Let's see if we can spell out the words *mom* and *love* by using our bodies to form letters. I need some volunteers to help spell out these words. Guide several volunteers to stand and use arms and legs to spell out the words.

God gives us moms, grandmothers, and other people in our lives to take good care of us.

What are some of the things your mom or others do to take care of you?

The Bible says in 1 John 4:12, "If we love one another, God lives in us and his love is made complete in us." This verse reminds us that each of us can show God's love to others.

Conclusion

Every day our moms and grandmothers and aunts show God's love by doing caring things for us. Let's thank God for them!

Close in prayer.

1 John 4:12

If we love one another, God lives in us and his love is made complete in us.

Going the Extra Mile

Activity

Give each student a sheet of paper and markers. *(Optional: Provide stickers and/or other decorating materials.)* **Today we're going to make awards for our moms or grandmothers or aunts or big sisters or any special person in our lives. These awards will help us say thank you to the special people who take care of us day after day.** Allow ten minutes to complete the task. As students make awards, they may tell to whom they are giving the awards. Volunteers can show their finished awards.

Bible Discussion

The Bible tells a story of a baby whose mom kept him safe when he could have been killed. Let's take a look at what Moses' mom did for him. Have a student read Exodus 2:1–10 aloud.

- **How would you describe Moses' mother's actions?**

- **What do these verses say about the actions of Moses' sister? Pharaoh's daughter?**

God gave Moses several women who cared for him: his mom, his sister, and Pharaoh's daughter.

Life Challenge

God knew we needed special people in our lives to care for us. We can show God our appreciation by thanking Him for our moms and others who show His love to us. Let's pray and thank God right now.

Prayer

Lord, thank You for Your love and for the people who show Your love to us. Show us ways to appreciate them every day. In Jesus' name. Amen.

Joy to the World

We can share the joy of Christmas with others.

Bible Talk

Let's pretend today is Christmas. On the count of three, I want you to get up and tell three people "Merry Christmas!" Ready? One ... two ... three! Allow time for students to complete the task. **Great job! You can sit down now.**

We usually only wish people a Merry Christmas at Christmastime, but the joy we feel at Christmas can be shared anytime. We can bring a Merry Christmas to everyone we come in contact with. What does the word *merry* mean? Allow time for volunteers to respond. **It means to be happy or full of joy. In Luke 2:10 angels told the shepherds the great news of Jesus' birth. The angel said to them, "Do not be afraid. I bring you good news that will cause great joy for all the people." What joyful news the shepherds received!**

As Christians, our role is the same as that of the angels in the story. God wants us to help people not to be afraid, but to hear and understand the joyful news of Jesus.

Conclusion

This Christmas, or even when it's not Christmas, we can be "angels" for others. In everything we do and say, we can let others see the joy we have because Jesus was born.

Close in prayer.

Luke 2:10

Do not be afraid. I bring you good news that will cause great joy for all the people.

Going the Extra Mile

Activity

Help students form groups of three to six and pick a leader for each group. **Today we are going to role-play. In your group, pretend you are a group of angels sent from God to tell the good news of Jesus to others. As angels, your goal is to convince me I can be joyful about Christmas. You can write a poem, sing a song, create a special poster, or do anything that will show me the joy of Jesus.** Provide the necessary supplies for the ideas you've suggested. Give the groups five to ten minutes to prepare. Then allow each group a chance to come to the front of the room and present their work. Be positive and thank them for the good news they've brought you. **Well done! You've really helped me discover the joy of Christmas.**

Bible Discussion

Let's take a more in-depth look at the angels who brought the good news to the shepherds. Have a student read Luke 2:8–20 aloud.

- **How can we be like angels to others this Christmas and help them discover the joy of Jesus' birth?**
- **What made the shepherds change from being afraid to being joyful and praising God?**

Life Challenge

Christmas brings lots of lights, toys, and parties, but the real joy of Christmas comes from celebrating Jesus' birth. When we help others remember that Christmas celebrates the good news of Jesus' birth, we can be like the angels who brought that good news to the shepherds. Our job is to bring great joy to everyone by showing them Jesus' love through what we say and how we act.

Prayer

Lord Jesus, thank You for the joy You bring to the world. Help us celebrate this Christmas by sharing joy with everyone around us. In Jesus' name. Amen.

Let's All Get Excited!

Jesus' resurrection brings great excitement to all who believe.

Bible Talk

Why do we celebrate Easter? Allow a few answers. If you had seen Jesus after His resurrection, how would you have reacted? Allow some answers. **I know I would be so excited, I'd just have to give a cheer! What sort of cheer would you give?** Allow several volunteers to demonstrate their cheers.

Then raise your hand in the air. **Let's all give together a great big "hooray" that Jesus is alive. When I put my hand down, give your best "hooray." When I put my hand back up, it's time to stop. Ready? One … two … three!** Lead children in cheering several times as you raise and lower your hand.

Conclusion

It's great to get excited about Easter. Jesus rose from the dead, and we can praise God for that! Mary Magdalene sure did. John 20:16 tells us that when she saw Jesus alive she called out, "Teacher!" Then she ran and told the disciples the good news. And here's what happened when Jesus' disciples first saw Him. Read John 20:19–20 aloud. **That's the sort of joy and excitement we can have at Easter and anytime we think about Jesus' resurrection.**

Close in prayer.

John 20:20
The disciples were overjoyed when they saw the Lord.

Going the Extra Mile

Activity

Some things in life may get some people excited, while those same things don't excite others at all. I'm going to list some situations. If the situation excites you, stand up. If it doesn't, then stay seated. Read each situation below, one at a time. After each situation, ask a person who stood why that situation is exciting. Then ask someone who didn't stand why the situation was not exciting.

Situations:

- Playing basketball
- Going to a play
- Eating steak for dinner
- Going to someone else's birthday party
- Playing a video game

Some of those situations excited you and some didn't. Each of us has different likes and dislikes. But the resurrection of Jesus is something we can all get excited about. Knowing Jesus is alive excites His followers more than anything else in the world!

Bible Discussion

The Bible tells us the great joy Jesus' followers had after His resurrection. Have a student or students read John 20:1–20 aloud.

- **How did the disciples feel at the beginning of this story? At the end of the story?**
- **What part of this story would you have most liked to see? Why?**

Life Challenge

We can all have the same overwhelming excitement as the disciples had. Jesus' empty tomb means just as much to us as it did to Jesus' early followers. We might be excited to go to a party or see a movie, but the joy of knowing Jesus is alive is something we can feel every day! Jesus is alive, so let's get excited!

Prayer

Jesus, You are the risen Savior. Thank You for dying on the cross for our sins. We are glad You are alive today! Help us show others our excitement about You. In Jesus' name. Amen.

Be Rich

We can be generous in doing kind things for others.

Bible Talk

What would you buy if you had $1? Allow time for students to respond. **What would you buy if you had $10?** Allow time for students to respond. Repeat the question-and-answer activity, increasing the amount of money each time.

How much money do you think you would need to have to be rich?

Sometimes it's fun to think about having a lot of money and what it would be like to be rich. The Bible talks about being rich too.

What do you think the Bible says we need in order to be rich?

First Timothy 6:18 says, "Command them to do good, to be rich in good deeds, and to be generous and willing to share." Everyone wants to be rich and have lots of money, but God wants us to be rich in another way. The Bible says when we are generous in being kind and treating others in good ways, it's like we're rich in good deeds.

Conclusion

Some people have a habit of counting their money every day. But instead of counting money, God wants us to count up our good actions—to find out if we're rich in the ways that help others.

Close in prayer.

1 Timothy 6:18
Command them to do good, to be rich in good deeds, and to be generous and willing to share.

Going the Extra Mile

Activity

Provide a whiteboard, dry-erase marker, and tennis ball. **Tabitha did good and kind things for others. In our game, we'll talk about good deeds that we can do for others. What are some good deeds we can do for others?** (listen to someone who has a problem, call someone who is sick, help someone with a hard chore, be friendly to a younger kid) List the responses on the board.

Choose one volunteer. The other students will stand in a large circle, spreading their legs so each student's right foot is touching the left foot of the next student. The volunteer stands in the middle of the circle. Give the ball to the volunteer.

I would like our volunteer to try as fast as possible to roll the ball toward people in the circle and try to get the ball between someone's legs. You may use your hands to swat away the ball, but you may not move your feet. If the ball gets past your legs, you must pantomime one of the good deeds on the list for others to guess. The first person to guess what the good deed is can have a turn to roll the ball. Lead students to play several rounds of the game. If the ball does not go through a student's legs after 30 seconds, call time and let any student pantomime a good deed.

Bible Discussion

The Bible tells us about a woman named Tabitha who was rich in good deeds. Let's read her story. Have a student read Acts 9:36–42 aloud.

- **What did Tabitha do to be rich in good deeds?**
- **Who are some people you know who are rich in good deeds?**
- **What is an example of a way someone your age can be rich in good deeds?**

It's not bad or wrong to have money, but it's even better to live generously in being kind and good.

Life Challenge

The Bible gives us lots of good examples of people who were rich in good deeds. And there are people in our lives who are generous in their kind and good actions. God can help each one of us be rich in good deeds!

Prayer

Father God, thank You for showing us how to be rich in deeds. Help us to do good and kind things for others. In Jesus' name. Amen.

Get Mad-Dog Mad

It's okay to get angry about injustice in the world.

Bible Talk

I know everyone here has been really angry at one time or another. Who would like to volunteer to show me what you do when you get angry? Allow a few volunteers to demonstrate their best show of anger. **You were really angry!**

Name some things you've been angry about. Is it ever good to get angry? Why or why not?

The Bible tells us about a time when Jesus was angry. Let's find out why. When Jesus entered the temple in Jerusalem, He found merchants cheating the people who had come to worship at the temple. The merchants were selling sick and injured animals for people to use as sacrifices to God. God's temple was for worship, and when Jesus saw the merchants cheating God's people, it made Him very angry. He got so angry He overturned the tables and drove the people out of the temple courts. He said, "My house is a house of prayer for all nations! But you have made it a hangout for robbers" (see Matthew 21:13). **Jesus saw a terribly unjust situation and got angry about it.**

God wants us to get angry too when we see injustice in the world. Read Micah 6:8 aloud. When we see bullies hurting others, it's okay to be angry. When we see Christians being selfish, it's okay to be upset. When we see people taking advantage of the poor, the sick, or the old, it's okay to be really mad.

Conclusion

As people who love Jesus, we can be angry when we see injustice. We can ask for God's help in knowing what to do to stop injustice in the world.

Close in prayer.

Micah 6:8

What does the Lord require of you? To act justly and to love mercy and to walk humbly with your God.

Going the Extra Mile

Activity

Let's pretend we are going to play a game. It doesn't matter what game we're going to play. What are some unfair ways to decide who goes first? Let several volunteers respond. **Now let's make a list of fair ways to see who goes first.** Let several volunteers respond. **If we were to play a game, and I chose one of the unfair ways to see who goes first, how would you feel?** Let several volunteers respond. **It feels terrible to be cheated or taken advantage of. As followers of Jesus, we can get angry and stand up against things that are unfair or unjust.**

Bible Discussion

The story of Jesus driving out people buying and selling in the temple is a great example of Jesus' anger at injustice. We can ask for God's help when we see others being taken advantage of. Help students form groups of three to six. **In your groups, think of some injustices or unfair situations that you've seen or heard about.** Give students five minutes and then have each group report. **There might be some unfair situations we can do something about. For example, if we know that there are hungry people in our town, we can collect food in our families and churches to share with them. Listen to what the Bible says about how we should act.** Read or invite a volunteer to read Micah 6:8 aloud.

- **What does this verse say about what God expects of His followers?**
- **What do you think it means to act justly? How might a kid your age act justly?**
- **How can God's followers show they love mercy?**

Life Challenge

In our lives there will be times when we can choose to treat others in fair ways. We can be ready for any opportunity to treat others with justice.

Prayer

Dear Jesus, thank You for showing us how important it is to treat others with justice. Help us to have the courage to stand up for what is right. In Jesus' name. Amen.

Help One Another

Jesus commands us to help each other.

Bible Talk

I want each of you to sit on the floor. Make sure your feet are flat on the ground and your knees are pulled up against your chest. Cross your arms around your chest. Now, while you are in that position, try and stand. Give students some time to try and get up. **Now find a partner of similar size as you and sit back-to-back in the same position. On the count of three, lean against each other and stand up. One … two … three!** Give everyone a chance to practice standing up. **Well done! You can all sit down now.**

Standing from that position is impossible by yourself. But with your partner's help, standing from that position went from impossible to being not so hard.

We can learn something from this exercise about how to live as followers of Jesus. It may seem really hard to follow Jesus' example every day. But when we help and serve one another, it is so much easier. We can pray for each other and help each other remember God's Word. Galatians 5:13 says, "Serve one another humbly in love." When we see others who are having a hard time following Jesus, we can become servants and help them. In the same way, they can do that for us too.

Conclusion

When we all help one another, following Jesus becomes much easier.

Close in prayer.

Galatians 5:13

Serve one another humbly in love.

Going the Extra Mile

Activity

Help students form groups of three to six, and then give each group paper and a pencil. **It is so important that each of us looks for ways to help one another follow Jesus' example. I would like each group to create a pact. Who can tell me what a pact is?** Allow students time to answer. **A pact is an agreement between two or more people to do something together or for one another. Using your pencil and paper, write a pact with your group. Your pact should tell one thing that every person in the group will do to help each other follow Jesus.** (pray for one another, memorize a Bible verse together) Give them about five minutes to create their pact. Then allow different groups to read aloud to the class what they wrote. **Good job, everyone. God wants us to help each other.**

Bible Discussion

The book of Galatians talks about being a helper, or a servant, to each other. Have a student read Galatians 5:13–15 aloud.

- **What's the main point of these verses?**
- **When is it easy for a kid your age to serve others? When might it be hard?**

The Galatians didn't seem to get along with each other very well. In his letter to them, Paul strongly urged them to serve one another and not to hurt each other. He told them to love each other as they love themselves, or else they would eventually destroy one another.

Life Challenge

These verses are good for us to remember too. When we serve each other by helping each other follow Jesus, we are all better able to show our love for God and others. If we're selfish and hurtful, others will have a hard time learning about God's love.

Prayer

Lord, teach us to serve You by serving each other. Show us ways to always help each other every day. In Jesus' name. Amen.

Look Out for Others

We can share God's love by looking for opportunities to help others.

Bible Talk

Let's play a game in which you have to look around the room to find something. Lead students in one or more of these games in which they look around the room to identify specific objects. *(Optional: Let students take turns leading the games.)*

I Spy Colors: Tell students the color of an item. ("I spy something blue.")

Higher or Lower: Tell students the position of an item. ("This object is higher than the window but lower than the ceiling.")

Size: Tell students the size of an item. ("This object is bigger than a book, but smaller than a table.")

You've done a good job of looking to find things in this room!

The Bible tells us about something else we can look for. Philippians 2:4 says, "[Don't be] looking to your own interests but ... to the interests of the others." This verse means we can care about the problems and needs of other people.

Conclusion

When we help others and care about them, we are showing God's love. So keep an eye out for the needs of others!

Close in prayer.

Philippians 2:4
[Don't be] looking to your own interests but ... to the interests of the others.

Going the Extra Mile

Activity

Help students form groups of three to six. Give each group a coin. **In your group, have one person toss the coin. If the coin lands heads up, each person in the group tells the name of someone they can help. If the coin lands tails up, each person in the group tells a way they can help someone.** Allow time for groups to repeat the activity several times. End the activity by asking groups to tell ways of helping others and looking out for their needs.

Bible Discussion

Sometimes we can help others easily and quickly—just by taking a few minutes of our time. And sometimes helping someone can take longer. Listen to this story in the Bible about a time four friends worked together to look out for the needs of another person. Have a student read Mark 2:1–12 aloud.

- **What made it difficult for the four men to take their friend to Jesus?**
- **Why do you think the four men didn't give up in bringing their friend to Jesus?**
- **When might a kid your age be able to help someone quickly and easily? When might it take longer and require more work?**

Even though it was hard work to carry their friend, the four men didn't give up. They did their best to help their friend.

Life Challenge

We show God's love for everyone when we care about the problems of others. Your friends might need your help when they are moving to a new neighborhood or when they have difficulty getting along with brothers and sisters. God helps us see when we can show His love to others.

Prayer

Lord, thank You that Your love is for everyone. Please help us look out for the needs of others and care about their problems. In Jesus' name. Amen.

Putting Others First

Jesus wants us to help and serve others.

Bible Talk

Let's get in a straight line as if we were going to march out of the room. Help get the children in line. **Who will be first in line?** Allow volunteers to respond. **Who will be last?** Allow volunteers to respond. **What if just outside the room, there was a plate of cookies, but only enough for some of you? How do you feel about where you are standing in line?** Allow several volunteers to answer. **It may seem unfair that those of you at the back of the line will either be last to get a cookie or may not even receive any cookie.**

When are some other times that kids your age line up in order to do something or receive something?

We might think the first person in line is the greatest, but Jesus said something different. In Mark 10:43, Jesus said, "Whoever wants to become great among you must be your servant." This verse means that if we help and serve others first—sometimes by letting them get in line before us—Jesus thinks we are great!

Conclusion

Jesus wants us to help and serve others as a way of sharing His love. In the times when it's hard to let someone else be first, remember to ask for God's help. And remember that Jesus thinks you're great!

Close in prayer.

Mark 10:43

Whoever wants to become great among you must become your servant.

Going the Extra Mile

Activity

Let's play a game in which we can put others first. Have all students take off their shoes and place them in a large pile in an open area to one side of the room. Group the students into equal teams at one end of the room. At the other end of the room, place several large sheets of paper (one for each team) and crayons on the floor. Assign each team a paper. **Find a partner in your team and then line up by pairs.** Help students form pairs within their teams and line up.

Hold up your arm. **When I lower my arm, the first pair from each team will run to your team's paper, trace each other's feet, and return to your team. After every member of your team has their feet traced, each pair of players will run to the shoe pile, find each other's shoes, and put the shoes on their partner's feet.** Play the game, repeating as time permits. **Thanks for serving and helping each other. I think you're great and Jesus does too!**

Bible Discussion

Let's see what happened when two of Jesus' disciples asked Him if they could be first. Have a student read Mark 10:35–45 aloud.

- **How would you describe Jesus' answer to James and John's request?**
- **What does Jesus say about Himself and serving others?**
- **When might it be hard for a kid your age to help and serve others first?**
- **When is a time you can put someone first?**

James and John didn't understand what it meant to be followers of Jesus. They didn't understand that following Jesus meant to help and serve others first.

Life Challenge

It can be hard to help and serve others before ourselves. Sometimes we may feel like we should help ourselves first. God understands when we feel that way. It's good to know we can pray and ask for God's help to show us ways to help others.

Prayer

Lord, thank You for the chance to serve and help others first. Help us to show Your love by putting others who are in need before ourselves. In Jesus' name. Amen.

Clothe Yourselves

As God's followers we can "put on," or show, kind and caring actions to others.

Bible Talk

Arrange chairs on two sides of the room. Create an aisle for volunteers to walk. **Today we're going to have a fashion show! In a fashion show people model clothes for others.** Choose three volunteers. **When I say "Start the show," one volunteer at a time will slowly walk down the aisle as if in a fashion show and then pose at the front of the room, facing the group.** Volunteers can begin the "fashion show." Narrate a fashion show commentary. Use the sample wording below to create comments for your show. Include a kind and caring action in each commentary.

Kelsey is wearing the latest trend in footwear. She is wearing blue sandals with a thin strap for a secure fit. These shoes were created just for Kelsey to walk to a friend's house to help the friend with homework. Thank you, Kelsey.

Max is wearing a dazzling shirt. He is wearing a mint-green button-down that screams, "I am fashion!" This shirt is the perfect color for Max to wear while he helps his grandfather. Thank you, Max.

Deidra is wearing a delicate sundress that is perfect for summer. This dress is appropriate for Deidra's summer picnics when she serves food to others. Thank you, Deidra.

That concludes our fashion show for today. Thank you, models. Encourage students to applaud.

Conclusion

Just like our models showed what they were wearing on the outside, our actions can show what we are like as followers of God. Instead of our being clothed with a dress or a shirt, the Bible tells us in Colossians 3:12 to "clothe yourselves with compassion, kindness, humility, gentleness and patience." This means that as followers of God, we can show, or "put on clothes of" kindness and caring.

Close in prayer.

Colossians 3:12

Clothe yourselves with compassion, kindness, humility, gentleness and patience.

Going the Extra Mile

Activity

Help students form groups of three to six. Pass out sheets of paper and markers or crayons. **I am going to give each group a kind and caring action from Colossians 3:12. In your groups, I'd like you to write a list of ways a kid your age can show the action you've been assigned. For example, if I assigned your group the word *patience*, your group would write ways that a kid your age can demonstrate patience to other people.** Assign an action to each group, repeating actions as needed. Then allow time for students to write their lists. Invite students to tell ideas to the whole class.

Bible Discussion

In the country of Judah, there lived an Israelite man with his wife, Naomi, and their two sons. When there was no food to eat in their country, they moved to the country of Moab. Then Naomi's husband died. The two sons married women of Moab, Ruth and Orpah. The two brides became part of the Israelite family and learned their husbands' way of life and faith in God. But then their husbands died too! Now all three of the women were widows. There was no one left to take care of them. So Naomi chose to return to her hometown in Judah. She hoped that her relatives back home would help her. Ruth went with Naomi, refusing to let her go alone. Knowing they needed to eat, Ruth volunteered to glean to get food for the two of them. Have a student read Ruth 2:6–7, 17–18 aloud.

- **What do Ruth's actions help you learn about her?**
- **Which word from Colossians 3:12 do you think best describes Ruth?**
- **When might you be kind and caring?**

Life Challenge

Ruth's kind and caring actions made a big difference in her life but also in the life of Naomi. Ruth had compassion for Naomi and showed kindness to her. We can show our love for others with our kind and caring actions.

Prayer

God, thank You for teaching us about compassion, kindness, humility, gentleness, and patience. Show us how to show love to others, using kind and caring actions. In Jesus' name. Amen.

Forgive Others

Because God first forgives us, we can forgive others.

Bible Talk

Have students stand in a circle. Turn to the student standing next to you and say, **I'm going to make a face that shows a feeling. I want you to pass that feeling to the next person in the circle by making the same face. Let's see how fast we can pass the feeling around the circle.** Make a face showing the feeling of excitement and allow time for students to pass the feeling around the circle. Repeat the activity, making faces that show sadness, boredom, fear, anger, and forgiveness. End the activity with anger and then forgiveness.

We did a good job of passing our feelings around the circle from one person to the next. Sometimes that is what happens in everyday life. If someone is feeling excited, others might feel excited too. The Bible tells us that we can pass forgiveness to others too. Ephesians 4:32 says, "Be kind and compassionate to one another, forgiving each other, just as in Christ God forgave you." Since God has loved us and forgiven us, He wants us to pass His love and forgiveness on to others.

Conclusion

Sometimes forgiving others isn't easy to do. None of us is perfect and we all make mistakes, but we can always ask for God's help to forgive someone else. We can keep the chain of forgiveness unbroken!

Close in prayer.

Ephesians 4:32

Be kind and compassionate to one another, forgiving each other, just as in Christ God forgave you.

Going the Extra Mile

Activity

Has anyone ever had to forgive someone or had to be forgiven? Allow a few volunteers to respond. **Let's play a game in which we forgive others. This game is like freeze tag. I need everyone to stand up and freeze in a position.** Demonstrate a frozen position. **When I count to three, I will tag someone to be the "Forgiver." The Forgiver will tag others and say "I forgive others" to unfreeze them. Once you have been tagged and forgiven, you become a Forgiver and can forgive others too. We'll play the game until everyone has been forgiven. Ready? One … two … three!** Allow a few minutes for children to play the game. **Fantastic! This was a fun game. In this game, forgiving others seemed easy, but sometimes forgiving others can be a hard thing to do.**

Bible Discussion

Have a student read Matthew 18:21–35 aloud.

- **How many times did Jesus tell Peter we should forgive others?**
- **Why do you think the servant did not forgive the other servant's debts?**
- **What does this story tell us about forgiveness?**

Even if someone tries to hurt our feelings or hurt our bodies, we can ask for God's help to know what to do and to forgive them.

Life Challenge

It's easier to forgive others when we remember God forgives us. We can do what the unforgiving servant did not do—forgive others.

Prayer

Lord, thank You for forgiving us when we do wrong things. Help us to forgive others who do wrong things. In Jesus' name. Amen.

Grow God's Fruit

As we grow the fruit of the Spirit in our lives, we show our love for God and others.

Bible Talk

Today let's play a game to see what kinds of fruit you like to eat. Help each student find a partner. One student chooses "odd" and the other chooses "even." **To play this game, put a hand behind your back.** Demonstrate actions as you describe them. **After I count to three, both of you bring out your hand with one to five fingers showing. If the total number of fingers is odd, the player who chose odd tells what kind of fruit he or she likes to eat. If the total is even, the other player tells an answer.** Lead students to play game several times. Students may find new partners between rounds. **The Bible talks about another kind of fruit. But instead of eating this fruit, we grow it!**

Galatians 5:22–23 says, "The fruit of the Spirit is love, joy, peace, forbearance, kindness, goodness, faithfulness, gentleness and self-control. Against such things there is no law." When Paul wrote these verses, he was comparing the way God's Spirit helps us grow good qualities in our lives to the way fruit grows. When we love Jesus, believe He is God's Son, and ask forgiveness for our sin, we can join God's family—and grow!

Conclusion

God gives the Holy Spirit to help us grow God's good fruit so we can show our love for God and others!

Close in prayer.

Galatians 5:22–23

The fruit of the Spirit is love, joy, peace, forbearance kindness, goodness, faithfulness, gentleness and self-control.

Going the Extra Mile

Activity

Help students form groups of three to six. Give each group paper and crayons or markers. **With your group, choose any kind of fruit.** Make sure each group chooses a different kind of fruit. **Have someone in your group draw a picture of the fruit on your group's sheet of paper. Label your fruit with a fruit of the Spirit we read about in Galatians 5:22–23.** *(Optional: Provide Bibles for children to read.)* **Then make a list of ways kids your age can show the fruit of the Spirit you chose.** Give groups five to seven minutes to work on the project. Then allow volunteers to read their lists.

When we first become members of God's family, we may not have grown very much of God's fruit. But as we grow and learn more about following God, He helps us grow His fruit.

Bible Discussion

Throughout the Bible we can read descriptions of how God wants us to grow as His followers. Sometimes it might seem like there are a lot of commands to remember! When Jesus lived on earth, He summarized the way we are to live. Ask a student to read Matthew 22:34–40 aloud.

- **How would you say these two commands in your own words?**

- **What is an example of how a kid your age might choose to show love for God? Love for others?**

- **What is one way you already show love for God and others? What is a new way you can obey these commands and show that you are growing God's fruit?**

Life Challenge

When Jesus lived on earth, He was a wonderful example of how to love God and others. As we grow God's fruit, we become more like Jesus. Every day we can depend on God to help us grow and grow!

Prayer

Lord, help us grow good fruit in our lives so that we can show our love for You and others. Thank You for giving us Your Holy Spirit to help us obey Your commands. In Jesus' name. Amen.

Humble Hearts

We can show God's love by being humble in the way we treat others.

Bible Talk

What do you think the word *humble* means? Allow a few volunteers to answer. **To be humble means to not think of yourself as better than other people. It means not being so proud of yourself that you don't care about others. What are some animals that remind you of being proud?** (Possible answers: eagle, peacock, lion) Allow a few volunteers to answer. **Let's walk around the room and act like animals who are proud.** Allow time for students to demonstrate the actions of proud animals. **What are some animals that remind you of being humble?** (Possible answers: cow, sheep, turtle) Allow a few volunteers to answer. **Let's walk around the room and act like animals who are humble.** Allow time for students to demonstrate the actions of humble animals. **Thank you, everyone.**

Let's talk about the times when we use the words *humble* and *proud* to describe people. People who are humble do not say or do things that make others feel bad about themselves. People who have pride boast that they are better than others because of their abilities. Because God loves us all the same, there's no reason for anyone to think they are better than someone else. Philippians 2:3 says, "Do nothing out of selfish ambition or vain conceit. Rather, in humility value others above yourselves." When we remember that God loves everyone, our humble attitudes help us not look down on others.

Conclusion

Instead of spending time comparing ourselves to others, we can think about God's love and how we can show His love to others—especially by our humble actions.

Close in prayer.

Philippians 2:3

Do nothing out of selfish ambition or vain conceit. Rather, in humility value others above yourselves.

Going the Extra Mile

Activity

Help students form pairs. **Today we're going to play a game in which we practice having humble attitudes by letting others go first.** Have pairs stand on one side of an open area in the room. Give each pair a sheet of paper. Partners should hold the paper between them, each with one hand on the paper. Pairs can practice stepping over the paper, one foot at a time, without letting go of the paper. At your signal, one student in each pair says "After you," and the partner takes a step, putting one foot and then the other over the paper. Then the partner who stepped says "After you," and the other partner takes a turn. Students continue in this manner, moving across the playing area and back. **Thank you for helping each other so well!**

Bible Discussion

Let's look at a story in the Bible that helps us learn more about what it means to be humble. Have a student read Luke 18:9–14 aloud.

- **Based on his prayer, what kind of person was the Pharisee?**
- **What do you think God thought of the Pharisee's prayer?**
- **Based on his prayer, what kind of person was the tax collector?**
- **What do you think God thought of the tax collector's prayer?**
- **How would you describe Jesus' comments about both prayers?**

Being humble is not something people talk much about. But our humble attitudes and actions are some of the best ways we can show God's love!

Life Challenge

When we have humble actions like the tax collector, we agree with God that we're not perfect and have done wrong things. When we ask God to forgive us, God is more than willing to forgive us and help us show His love to others by our humble attitudes and actions. Let's pray and thank God for showing us how to be humble.

Prayer

Lord, thank You for showing us in the Bible how to be humble. Help us to show Your love to others by our humble attitudes and actions. In Jesus' name. Amen.

Let's All Get Along

God wants us to do our best to get along with each other and not argue.

Bible Talk

I'm going to divide you up into two teams: boys on one side and girls on the other. We're going to find out who is better: boys or girls. Boys, when I point to your group, yell "Boys rule!" Girls, when I point to your group, yell "Girls rule!" Ready? Alternate back and forth, pointing to the two groups a few times. **Thank you. Both groups did a great job!**

It's fun to shout back and forth in a contest. But it's pretty silly to argue over who's better. Sometimes people—boys and girls and grown-ups—get into arguments over silly things.

Second Timothy 2:23 says, "Don't have anything to do with foolish and stupid arguments, because you know they produce quarrels." This verse is a message to all of us to try our very best to get along and cooperate with each other.

Conclusion

Getting involved in silly arguments can sometimes cause big fights and keep us from showing God's love to others. So let's ask God to help us get along with each other.

Close in prayer.

2 Timothy 2:23
Don't have anything to do with foolish and stupid arguments, because you know they produce quarrels.

Going the Extra Mile

Activity

Help children form groups of three to six. Try to group the children by height in order to make the game work. **We're going to play a game in which cooperation is very important. Each group needs enough room to make a very tight circle. Turn so your left shoulder is pointing toward the middle of the circle, and make your circle as tight as possible. Now, slowly on the count of three, sit down on the lap of the person behind you. One ... two ... three ... sit! Now that you're sitting on the lap of the person behind you, on the count of three try and walk—using your inside leg first. One ... two ... three! Good work, everyone!** Have the students take their seats again.

- **Was it easy or difficult to walk together?**
- **What happened when you or someone else got out of step?**
- **What can this game teach us about working together as Christians?**

Bible Discussion

In the Bible, we can see how important it was for people to get along. Paul knew this too, and in a letter to Timothy he explained the importance of getting along with others. Have a student read 2 Timothy 2:22–24 aloud.

- **What are some of the commands you read in these verses?**
- **When might one of the commands help a kid your age?**

Timothy was a young pastor of a church, and Paul was his mentor, or teacher. Times were hard for Paul and for other Christians. Bad government leaders and false teachers did not want people to become Christians. While Paul was in prison, other Christians were being hurt and sometimes killed for following Jesus. The importance of Christians getting along could not have been greater. That's why Paul told Timothy to make sure his church did not get involved in foolish and stupid arguments. He told them not to argue with each other and to be kind to everyone. No matter what situations we're in, we can obey this command to show God's love.

Life Challenge

When our words and actions show God's love, it helps everyone around us learn more about God and His love for them. Our kind actions not only help our lives to be better, but they can make a big difference in the lives of others too.

Prayer

Lord, help us to get along and not argue about silly things. Show us how to work together so that we can show everyone Your love. In Jesus' name. Amen.

Listening to Each Other

We can show God's love by being good listeners.

Bible Talk

Think about your favorite place to eat. On the count of three, I would like each of you to turn and face a person sitting next to you. Tell that person about your favorite place to eat and why you like eating there. Ready? One … two … three! Allow time for students to complete the task. **Thank you.**

Raise your hand if you think your neighbor heard what you said. You may have been able to hear your neighbor's voice, but you probably weren't able to really listen to each other.

Why do you think it may have been hard for you to listen to one another? (too many people talking at the same time, the person next to me was trying to talk and listen at the same time, some people talking louder than others)

When everyone talks at once, no one is able to really listen and focus on what each person is saying. James 1:19 says, "My dear brothers and sisters, take note of this: Everyone should be quick to listen, slow to speak and slow to become angry." This verse tells us we should listen to each other first before speaking ourselves.

When we listen to others, we give them our full attention. That means we are able to look them in the eyes and understand their feelings when they speak, and then we're able to respond to whatever they say.

Conclusion

Listening to others is one of the best ways we can show God's love.

Close in prayer.

James 1:19
Take note of this: Everyone should be quick to listen, slow to speak and slow to become angry.

Going the Extra Mile

Activity

I would like to tell you a story about something important to me. Briefly tell a personal story that has meaning to you. It could be the story of your baptism, when you got a special birthday or Christmas gift, or when your family took a vacation. Be sure to include in your story answers to the questions below.

Now I'm going to ask you some questions about the story to see if you were really listening. Ask four to five questions.

- **What was the special event I told about?**
- **How did I feel about the event? Why?**
- **What is one choice I made in this story? Why did I make that choice?**
- **How did the story end?**

You are great listeners! You made me feel that what I had to say was important and you cared about my story. God is a very good listener too. We can show God's love to others simply by being good listeners!

Bible Discussion

Have a student read James 1:19–20 aloud. **James, the man who wrote these verses, was the half brother of Jesus and a follower of Jesus. James wanted the people who loved Jesus to also show love to each other. When James wrote this letter, Christianity was drawing in people from different cultures, with different ideas and beliefs. Jesus' followers had to learn to get along with each other.**

- **What commands are in these verses?**
- **When is a time that kids need to listen to each other?**
- **What is something kids can do to show that they are slow to become angry?**

James knew that if all Christians listened to one another, then they would show God's love and not argue and become angry.

Life Challenge

We can learn from what James said too. This week at home, at school, or even at church, practice listening before speaking to others. Remember, when we are good listeners we show God's love to others.

Prayer

Lord, thank You for showing us how to listen to others. Help us to show Your love by being good listeners. In Jesus' name. Amen.

Love Fulfills the Law

Loving each other is a very important rule God gives us.

Bible Talk

Let's pretend we're getting ready to take a road trip. We need to make up some rules for the trip. What are some rules that, if followed, will make the trip fun for everyone? (make sure to have a map, no snoring when you're asleep, everyone bring a toothbrush, no one can use the restroom until we get to our destination) **Those rules are great. Did you know we could eliminate all our rules for the trip except for one? The rule that we can't get rid of is "Love your neighbor as yourself."**

When Jesus lived on earth, He was asked what someone had to do to inherit eternal life—to live with God forever. Jesus answered by giving two commands: love God and love others (see Luke 10:27). **When Jesus was commanding us to love others, He said, "Love your neighbor as yourself."**

What do you think it means to love someone else as much as you love yourself?

When we love one another, we are able to share God's love with them. This means we can say and do kind things for others and treat everyone with respect.

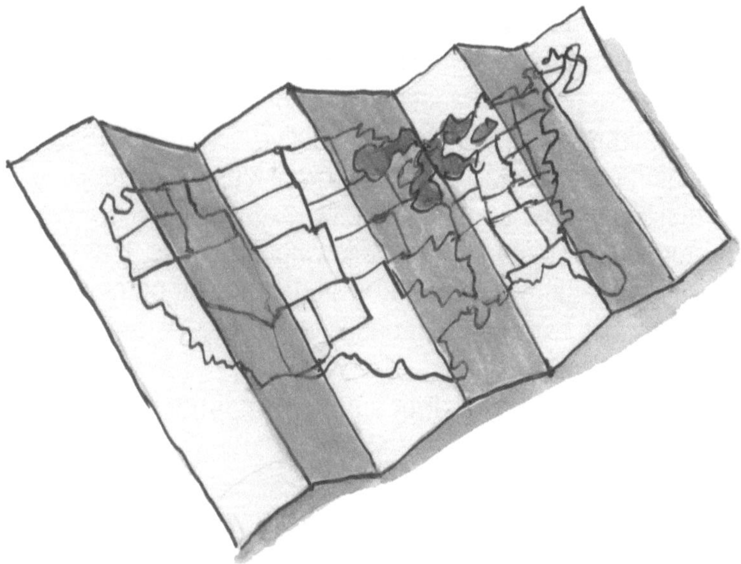

Conclusion

Loving each other is the most important rule that God gives us in the Bible about how to treat others. When we follow that rule, even a trip to the grocery store will work out fine!

Close in prayer.

Luke 10:27
Love your neighbor as yourself.

Going the Extra Mile

Activity

Using one chair for every two students, put chairs in a circle, facing out, and with some space between the chairs. Number sheets of paper according to how many chairs you have. Place one sheet of paper on each chair. **To begin this game, I would like two students to sit on each chair. Now listen and follow the directions: If you are wearing blue, move two chairs to the left.** Pause while students follow the directions. Then call out a number. The student(s) sitting on that chair tell about a way kids can love their neighbors as much as they love themselves. Repeat the game with the following directions. If at any point there are too many students to sit on one chair, they may put their hands on the chair.

If you came to church in a car, move three chairs to the right.

If you ate cereal for breakfast, move one chair to the right.

If you made your bed this morning, move two chairs to the left.

Repeat the game as time permits.

Bible Discussion

Let's talk some more about following Jesus' command to love others. Have a student read Romans 13:8–10 aloud.

- **What's the main idea of these verses?**
- **Why might it be hard for a kid your age to show love to someone?**

Paul, the author of these verses and a follower of Jesus, understood that love is the main thing we must keep doing for one another. Paul said love fulfills the law (see Romans 13:10), **which means when we choose to love each other, we are doing just what God's law in the Old Testament wants us to do.**

Life Challenge

One of the best things about showing love to others is we don't have to wait for others to go first! We can start by being kind and loving to others before they start being loving and kind to us. We can set an example for others to follow. Let's make a pledge today that we will follow God's important rule—to love one another.

Prayer

Dear God, thank You for loving us so much. Help us to share Your love with others. In Jesus' name. Amen.

Love Your Enemies

Jesus wants us to love our enemies.

Bible Talk

Who would like to imitate a famous bad guy (Goliath, Lex Luthor, Darth Vader) **from a book or movie?** Allow a few volunteers to show off their imitations of villains. **Those imitations were terrific! Sometimes when we hear the word *enemy*, we think of people like these villains. But in everyday life, kids your age have people who might seem like an enemy. Maybe it's a teacher you see as unfair, or a classmate who is always annoying you or picking on you.**

When there is someone who doesn't seem to like you, how do you feel like acting?

What's some advice you've heard about how to treat an enemy?

In Mathew 5:44, Jesus told us how to treat our enemies. He said, "I tell you, love your enemies and pray for those who persecute you." It would be so much easier if Jesus had asked us to FIGHT our enemies! He could have even asked us to ignore them or stay away from them. But instead Jesus told us to love them and pray for them! We might think, *Anything but that!* But that's exactly what Jesus commands us to do because of His great love for all people.

Conclusion

We can show our enemies Jesus' love. Think of someone you need to love and pray for. Let's do what Jesus says and pray for our enemies right now.

Close in prayer.

Matthew 5:44

I tell you, love your enemies and pray for those who persecute you.

Going the Extra Mile

Activity

Let's pretend I'm the most disliked kid in school. I cut in line. I steal all the time. I say mean and hurtful things to people. I cheat on tests. I ruin playground time by picking fights. No one likes me, and I don't like anyone!

- **How would I probably be treated at your school?**
- **What if everyone started treating me like Jesus commanded? What if everyone in my class treated me with love and prayed for me?**

Choose one volunteer. **If I was your enemy, show me how you would treat me if you obeyed Jesus' commands.** Allow a few seconds for the student to demonstrate actions. **Jesus wants us to treat everyone with love and kindness, including those who are really hard to love.**

Bible Discussion

In the Bible, we can see that Jesus did what He told others to do. Have a student read Luke 23:33–35 aloud. **Even when Jesus was killed, He loved those who were killing Him! He asked God to forgive them. It's hard to imagine such amazing love for an enemy!**

- **What makes it so hard for us to love our enemies and pray for them?**
- **What can we do when we need to keep loving our enemies?**
- **Who can we ask to help us plan how to handle an enemy?**

Life Challenge

Getting along with other people isn't always easy. Even the best of friends have times when they feel upset or angry at each other. And when people are mean to us, those upset or angry feelings are even worse. Loving our enemies doesn't happen automatically. Jesus knows the difficult situations we might be in, and He wants us to ask Him for help as we obey His command to love our enemies.

Prayer

Lord Jesus, help us follow Your example and love our enemies. When we are tempted to be mean to people who have hurt us or have been mean to us, help us remember to show Your love. Thank You for always being with us to give us strength to do what is right. In Jesus' name. Amen.

Serving with Our Abilities

We can use our abilities and talents to serve God.

Bible Talk

What are abilities and talents? Allow a few answers. **Abilities and talents are special characteristics God gives us. For example, being able to write poetry or play basketball is an ability that God gives us. Today we'll pantomime—act without speaking—some of our abilities. As each ability is pantomimed, try to guess what the ability is. I need one volunteer.** Choose a volunteer. _____ (name of volunteer) **is going to whisper an ability or talent for me to act out for you. Let's see if you can guess what it is.** Let the volunteer whisper an ability to you. Act out the ability for children to guess. **Good job! Now I need some more volunteers.** Choose several volunteers. **I will whisper an ability or talent to each of them.** One at a time, have the volunteers take turns acting out abilities for the other students to guess. Continue as time permits.

God made each of us unique by giving us all different abilities. Some people can sing, some people can dance, some people are good at math, and some people are good spellers. No matter what your ability is, you can use it to serve God. In the Bible, Colossians 3:23 says, "Whatever you do, work at it with all your heart, as working for the Lord, not for human masters." This verse means that no matter what we do, whether it's playing soccer or singing a song, we should do the best job we can because we're doing it for God.

Conclusion

God wants us to get better at using our abilities and then use them to serve God and share His love with others.

Close in prayer.

Colossians 3:23

Whatever you do, work at it with all your heart, as working for the Lord, not for human masters.

Going the Extra Mile

Activity

Pass out large sheets of paper and markers or crayons. **Today we'll make posters by creating our own word slogans to encourage people to use their possessions and unique abilities God has given them. For example, you could make up a word slogan like "Use It or Lose It" or "Give It Your Best." Write your slogan on your sheet of paper and then decorate it.** *(Optional: Students could cut out letters from magazines and glue the letters to paper to make slogans.)* Allow up to 15 minutes to complete the task. Invite students to show their posters.

Bible Discussion

In the Bible, Jesus told a story about three men who were given different amounts of gold. They each used their gold in different ways. Let's find out what happened. Have a student read Matthew 25:14–25 aloud. *(Optional: Assign students to read the parts of the master and the three servants.)*

- **According to these verses, what did the first man do with his gold? The second man? The third man?**
- **What did Jesus want us to learn from this story?**
- **How might a kid your age "bury" something he or she owns or some ability he or she has—instead of using it? How might that kid make good use of that same thing?**

As we share the possessions God gave us and use the abilities God gave us, we can show how much we love and thank God for what He's given to us.

Life Challenge

God loves us all the same, but He also gave each of us different ways to serve Him and share His love with others. Whatever God has given you—put your best effort into using it for God.

Prayer

God, thank You for giving us all abilities and talents. Thank you for everything you give us. Show us how to serve You by sharing with others—and not burying what we have. In Jesus' name. Amen.

True Friendship

True friends show God's love no matter what.

Bible Talk

I'm going to read a list of situations about friends. If you agree with the situation, give a thumbs-up. Demonstrate the action. **If you do not agree with the situation, give a thumbs-down.** Demonstrate the action. Then read the following list, pausing after each situation for students to demonstrate a thumbs-up or thumbs-down.

I would go to Disneyland with my friend.

I would go to the library with my friend.

I'd help my friend take out the trash.

I'd share ice cream with my friend.

I'd go to a sleepover at my friend's house.

I'd help my friend practice kicking a soccer ball.

We all like to have friends, and it's fun to do things with them. Part of being a good friend to someone means doing something with your friend or helping your friend, even when it's not your favorite thing to do. That's what the Bible talks about in Proverbs 17:17: "A friend loves at all times." True friends help one another and show God's love to one another, no matter what situation they are in.

Conclusion

Every day your friends can show that they care about you, and you can show that you care about them. It's great to have true friends!

Close in prayer.

Proverbs 17:17
A friend loves at all times.

Going the Extra Mile

Activity

Help students pair up. Pass out sheets of paper and pencils to each pair. **In your pairs, I'd like you to write two situations in which friends may not get along. For example, it may be hard for friends to get along if a friend cheats on homework using another friend's answers.** Allow a few minutes for students to complete the task. **Now I'd like you to trade your paper with another pair. Read the situations on the new paper and write suggestions for what friends could say or do to get along in each situation.** Allow a few minutes to complete the task. Invite students to share their work. **Excellent! Those are great ideas for how to be true friends.**

Bible Discussion

Let's read about an example of true friendship in the Bible. Saul was the king of Israel, and Jonathan was his son, a prince. David was a young shepherd who lived in the country. After David defeated Goliath, King Saul brought David to his palace to live with him. During that time, Jonathan and David became very good friends. Have a student read 1 Samuel 18:1–4 aloud.

- **What did Jonathan give to David as a sign of friendship?**

Have a student read 1 Samuel 19:1–7 aloud.

- **What choice did Jonathan have to make?**
- **How did Jonathan keep his promise of friendship to David?**

David and Jonathan made a promise to remain true friends. David and Jonathan showed that they cared for one another, and Jonathan stood up for David in a difficult time.

Life Challenge

It's easy to choose to be a true friend when your friend wants to give you a present or take you someplace special. But even in difficult times, when your friend needs your help, God wants you to show love and care. True friends care for each other in good and bad situations. Let's thank God for the true friends we have.

Prayer

God, thank You for giving us true friends. Show us how to love and care for our friends, no matter what happens. In Jesus' name. Amen.

Watch What You Say

We can show God's love by being careful of what we say.

Bible Talk

The tongue is an interesting part of the body. We can do all kinds of interesting things with it! When I give the signal, let's see what creative and silly things you can do with your tongue. You can stick out your tongue to see how far it goes, or try to roll your tongue like a scroll, or you could even try to touch your chin with your tongue! Ready? One … two … three! Give students a few minutes to experiment. **Cool! You were able to do all types of things!**

We use our tongues for several things but mainly to speak. Without the tongue, we would not be able to speak a word! The Bible says in Ephesians 4:29, "Do not let any unwholesome talk come out of your mouths, but only what is helpful for building others up according to their needs." Unfortunately, some things we say can be mean and hurtful to others, but this verse tells us the words we say can make a big difference in the lives of others. We can help others or hurt them—the choice is ours!

Conclusion

Every day as you use your tongue to help you eat and to help you talk, remember to use your tongue to follow God's command to say good things.

Close in prayer.

Ephesians 4:29

Do not let any unwholesome talk come out of your mouths, but only what is helpful for building others up.

Going the Extra Mile

Activity

Help students form groups of three to six. Give each group paper and pencils. **In your groups, I'd like you to think of situations in which you have to choose what kinds of words to use. Write brief descriptions of the situations, using the sentence starter "What do you say when ...?"** Allow a few minutes for discussion and writing. Then collect each group's papers. Read each question aloud and ask volunteers to suggest answers. Discuss the answers.

- **What else might you say?**
- **What might result from your words?**

Good job, everyone. You've thought of some good situations in which we can remember to obey Ephesians 4:29. Read the verse aloud.

Bible Discussion

Let's look at what James, a follower of Jesus, had to say about the power of our words. Have a student read James 3:3–12 aloud.

- **What does James compare the tongue to?**
- **If James was writing today, what small things might he compare the power of a tongue to?**
- **How might one unkind or hurtful word start a lot of trouble?**

Even though the tongue is one of the smallest body parts, it can cause the biggest problems! When we say unkind things about someone, we have the ability to hurt that person's feelings—and we show God that we don't care about treating people right.

Life Challenge

Starting today, let's think about how we can better control our tongues and speak kind words to others. Even if you face a mean person or someone who says unkind things about you, you can still model Jesus' example and show others how to watch what they say.

Prayer

God, forgive us for any unkind words we've said to people. Thank You for showing us how to properly use our tongues. In Jesus' name. Amen.

Be Prepared

We can be prepared to tell about our faith in God.

Bible Talk

I am going to ask you several questions. When you have the answer, walk quickly to the front of the room and call out the answer. Then return to your seats for the next question. As you ask each of the following questions, pause after each one for students to respond. Adapt questions according to the ability level of your students.

What is 10 x 10?

How many states are in the United States of America?

What is the law called that means that objects fall to the ground?

In math, there is addition, subtraction, multiplication, and what else?

Is Earth a planet or a star?

Where did you learn the answers to those questions? Allow students to respond. **Allow students to respond. The answers to those questions are facts. There was only one answer for each question. You most likely learned the answers to the questions from a teacher or a book. Because you studied and learned the answers, you were prepared to give the right answers to the questions.**

The Bible tells us we can be prepared in another way. First Peter 3:15 says, "Always be prepared to give an answer to everyone who asks you to give the reason for the hope that you have." This verse means we can study and learn to answer questions about our faith in God. When others ask us questions about God, we can give them answers that are facts. Facts about God are found in the Bible.

Conclusion

It's not a very good feeling when we're asked a question and don't know what the answer is. Reading and studying God's Word not only helps us learn what is true about God, but it helps us be prepared to give others the right answers about believing in God.

Close in prayer.

1 Peter 3:15

Always be prepared to give an answer to everyone who asks you to give the reason for the hope that you have.

Going the Extra Mile

Activity

Write the words *God*, *Jesus*, *Prayer*, and *Bible*, one each, at the top of four large sheets of paper. Help students form groups of three to six. Give markers to the students. **In your group, think of something you've learned—a fact—about each of these items. For example, you might say, "God created the world" as a fact about God. After you've thought of at least one fact for each item, the people in your group may take turns writing the facts on the sheets of paper.** Allow time to complete the task. Provide help as needed. When time is up, read the sentences on each paper aloud.

Bible Discussion

One of Jesus' followers was a man named Paul. Let's find out what Paul told others about his belief in God. Have a student read Acts 17:18–20, 22–24.

- **What question did the people listening to Paul ask him?**

- **What did Paul say about Jesus? About God?**

Later in Acts 17, we read that some of the people listening to Paul chose to believe in Jesus and become Jesus' followers (v. 34). **Because Paul was ready to tell about God, he helped others become members of God's family.**

Life Challenge

Telling others what we believe about God may not be an easy thing to do. But it's good to know that just like we can study math problems or spelling words to learn those things, we can read and study God's Word to learn about Him. The more we learn about God, the more we can be prepared to share the good news of His love and power with others.

Prayer

Thank You, God, for Your Word. Help us to be prepared to share our beliefs about You with others. In Jesus' name. Amen.

Don't Stop the Chain

We can help spread the good news about Jesus' love.

Bible Talk

Ask six to eight volunteers to stand in a straight line. **I'm going to tell the first person in line a true statement. Then I want you to say the statement to the person next to you, and on down the line to the last person. Here's the statement: "Jesus loves you!"** Give the children a chance to pass the statement down the line. **Good work! Everyone in the line got to hear the good news that Jesus loves them. Let's do it again.** This time after they start, stop them at about the third or fourth child. **This time I stopped you. Raise your hand if you didn't get to hear the good news. No one past this point got to hear the very important good news.**

What can this game teach us? Wait for some answers. **Every time we don't tell others with our words and actions about Jesus and His love, someone else doesn't get a chance to hear the greatest news in the world. Just like in our chain, once the news wasn't passed on anymore, no one else got the message. But we can tell everyone the good news about Jesus! That's why 2 Timothy 4:2 says, "Preach the word; be prepared in season and out of season." We must be urgent about telling everyone about Jesus.**

Conclusion

We can keep from breaking the chain. If we tell the good news whenever we can, more and more people will hear the good news about Jesus' great love.

Close in prayer.

2 Timothy 4:2

Preach the word; be prepared in season and out of season.

Going the Extra Mile

Activity

Divide groups into two teams. Ask one team to stand in the middle of the room. Divide the other team in half and ask each half to stand on opposite sides of the room. To the half team on one end of the room hand a paper that says "Jesus loves you!"

In our first activity, we had a chain of people telling the good news that "Jesus loves you!" This time the good news is in the form of a note. The half team on this end of the room must get the message to their teammates on the other side of the room, while the team in the middle tries to stop them. Here are the rules: (1) Teams can't touch each other. (2) The team trying to get the message across the room must stay on their assigned end of the room. (3) If the team in the middle intercepts the message, the message goes back to the beginning for another try.

Encourage the half team trying to get the message across the room to be creative. For example, they may want to make an airplane out of the paper. Or they may want to crumple the paper into a ball and throw it. If you have time, switch roles and let the team in the middle be on the outside.

That was a terrific effort to get such an important message across the room to your teammates! But the team in the middle made it really hard to get the message across.

- **What are some things that may stop you from sharing the good news about Jesus with others?**

- **Who has told you the good news about Jesus?**

- **Who are some people you can tell about Jesus' love?**

Bible Discussion

In 2 Timothy, Paul, a follower of Jesus, encouraged a young pastor named Timothy to be urgent in spreading the good news of Jesus. Have a student read 2 Timothy 4:1–5 aloud. **When Paul was alive, Christianity had not yet been well established and many people did not want Jesus' teachings to spread. So when Paul told Timothy to be urgent in spreading the good news of Jesus, he knew the growth of Christianity depended on sharing the gospel. Paul wanted the gospel to be shared from one person to the next.**

Life Challenge

Just like people in the Bible who urgently shared the good news, we can do the same.

Prayer

Dear God, thank You for sending Jesus to show us Your love. Help us to share Jesus' love with everyone. In Jesus' name. Amen.

Fishers of Men

We can be ready to follow Jesus and help others learn about Him.

Bible Talk

Let's go fishing today. Everyone will need a fishing pole and some bait. Let's connect our bait to the fishing poles. Pretend to connect bait to the end of a fishing pole. Have the children imitate your actions. **Now let's cast our fishing lines out into the sea.** Pretend to cast, and wait for a few seconds. **Wait a minute! I think we may have caught something! Let's reel in our lines.** Pretend to reel in. **It's a swordfish! That's a pretty big fish. Let's try to catch something else.** Keep pretending to catch things (whale, shark, goldfish, boot, etc). End by expressing great surprise when you catch a person. **When we go fishing, we don't fish for people. But that's what Jesus said in Matthew 4:19 that He would help us do. "Come, follow me," Jesus said, "and I will send you out to fish for people."**

When Jesus said that, He didn't mean we would catch people like we catch fish. He meant we would help others learn about Him by what we say and do. And we would bring them "in" as His followers.

Conclusion

When we share the love of Jesus with everyone we meet, we help others become followers of Jesus too.

Close in prayer.

Matthew 4:19

"Come, follow me," Jesus said, "and I will send you out to fish for people."

Going the Extra Mile

Activity

We're going to play a game called Fish for People. I will need two volunteers to be fishermen. Choose two volunteers. **When I say "Go," I want everyone to get up and walk around the room. Our two fishermen will close their eyes and walk around the room while saying, "Fish!" The rest of you will respond, "For people!" The fishermen will try to follow the voices and tag everyone else. Once you are tagged, you become a fisherman and try to tag someone else. Ready to play? Go!** Play several rounds, choosing different volunteers to be fishermen each time.

Bible Discussion

Have a student read Matthew 4:18–22 aloud.

- **Why do you think the men in these verses decided to follow Jesus?**
- **What does it mean for a kid your age to follow Jesus?**
- **When might it be hard for a kid your age to follow Jesus? When might it be easy?**

Life Challenge

The men who followed Jesus that day became His disciples. They shared Jesus' love with many people, and because of them many people believed in Jesus. We can be ready to follow Jesus and help others learn about Him, just like the disciples did.

Prayer

Dear God, thank You for choosing us to follow You. Help us to share everything we know about You with others. In Jesus' name. Amen.

Lighting Up the World

Our words and actions can help others see how great and loving God is.

Bible Talk

Think of an object that shines light, but don't say the object's name aloud. When you've thought of something, raise your hand. Ask a student with a raised hand to stand in front of the group and pantomime using the item. Other students guess the item. Repeat with other volunteers.

What are some of the ways in which lights help us?

Lights can make a big difference in helping people know where to go and see what's important. The Bible tells us that people in God's family are like lights. Matthew 5:16 says, "Let your light shine before others, that they may see your good deeds and glorify your Father in heaven." When we obey God with our words and actions, we are like lights. We help other people see how great and loving God is.

Conclusion

Jesus calls His followers "the light of the world" (Matthew 5:14). **As you spend time with your family and your friends, think about how your words and actions can be like lights to help them see God!**

Close in prayer.

Matthew 5:16
Let your light shine before others, that they may see your good deeds and glorify your Father in heaven.

Going the Extra Mile

Activity

Spread out a large sheet of paper on the floor. Draw lines on the paper to divide it into eight or ten sections. **Raise your hand if you can think of an action that can show you want to love and obey God.** Have children who respond write the actions in different sections of the paper. After sections have been filled, have a volunteer stand several feet away, at a designated spot, and toss a coin or beanbag onto the paper. Read aloud the action that was hit.

- **When is a time someone your age could show this action and be a light to help others see God?**

Repeat the activity as time permits, or until each student has had a turn.

Bible Discussion

Let's discover some more good things that happen when we obey Jesus' command to be the light of the world. Have a student read Matthew 5:13–16 aloud.

- **How is doing good things like being a light?**
- **What can others see when we do good things because we love God?**
- **What are some words or actions you can say and do to show what God is like?**

Jesus' words in this Scripture remind us that if we aren't acting as the light of the world, it's as if the world is dark—people aren't able to see who God is and what He is like.

Life Challenge

Sometimes it's easy for us to think that our words and actions don't really make much of a difference. Kids might think they are too young to really make something change. But even if we don't see the results, our small actions can make a difference—just like even a small light can help us see in the darkness. So get out there and light up your school, your neighborhood, your dance class, or your soccer team!

Prayer

Dear God, help us look for ways every day in which our words and actions can shine like lights so others can see how great and loving You are. In Jesus' name. Amen.

Tell the Good News

We can share the good news of Jesus with everyone.

Bible Talk

Let's pretend someone you know is very sick. Suddenly, you discover there is a cure for this terrible illness. What would the headline in a newspaper say? Allow several volunteers to answer. **Now let's pretend you've been given some really cool toys to give to kids who have no toys. What would the headline in a newspaper say?** Allow several volunteers to respond. As time permits, suggest several other examples of good news.

We have some wonderful news we can deliver to others every day. What do you think it is? Allow time for volunteers to respond. **The love of Jesus is wonderful news the whole world needs to hear. Jesus commands us to tell this news. Jesus says in Matthew 28:19, "Go and make disciples of all nations."**

Conclusion

We can deliver the good news of Jesus every single day by showing others Jesus' love in what we say and do.

Close in prayer.

Matthew 28:19

Go and make disciples of all nations.

Going the Extra Mile

Activity

Let's play a game to see how fast we can tell the good news about Jesus. I will be the announcer. When I say "Go and make disciples," I want you to walk around the room. When I say "Tell the good news," I want you to stop walking, spin around, and sit down on the floor as quickly as possible. The first person to sit down gets to tell everyone something he or she knows about Jesus. For example, you might say, "Jesus cares for us." Play the game for several rounds. *(Optional: For each round, name a new action that students need to do when the announcement is made. For example, do a jumping jack before sitting down, or place hands on head while spinning before sitting down.)* **Wasn't that fun? Let's see what the Bible says about telling others the good news of Jesus.**

Bible Discussion

In the Bible, Jesus commands us to tell the good news to the world. Have a student read Matthew 28:16–20 aloud.

- **What promise does Jesus give along with the command?**
- **What do you think it means to make someone a disciple of Jesus?**
- **Is it hard or easy for kids your age to obey Jesus' command in these verses? Why?**

Jesus wants all of us to follow Him. Before we can follow Jesus, we have to hear about Him first. We can tell others about Jesus' love so they can become followers of Jesus too.

Life Challenge

God has given us a fantastic gift to share with everyone. God loved us so much that His Son, Jesus, died for our sins and rose again. The story of Jesus is a gift that can be shared with everyone. We can share it by what we say, how we act, how we help others, and how we care for others. When we do this, we share the great gift that God has given us.

Prayer

Lord, thank You for sending Jesus to die for our sins. Help us to share the good news of Jesus with everyone. In Jesus' name. Amen.

What Would You Say?

We can be ready to speak the good news about Jesus.

Bible Talk

What kinds of things would you say if you were a pirate? Allow students to respond by saying things like "Argh!" or "Yo ho ho." Then ask the same question as you name, one at a time, the following kinds of people; pause after each one for students to respond: cheerleader, football player, waiter, judge, teacher. **You've done a good job speaking like all these people. But what do you think you would say if someone asked you to speak as a witness for Jesus?**

We can be ready to say things to others about what Jesus is like and the wonderful things He has done. Acts 22:15 says, "You will be his witness to all people of what you have seen and heard." This verse tells us WE are the people that God wants to tell others about Jesus' love. We can be ready to speak the good news about Jesus to anyone we meet.

Conclusion

All of us are going to have different jobs when we grow up. Not all of us are going to be teachers or cheerleaders or football players. But we can all be witnesses for Jesus—and we don't have to wait until we grow up to speak as His witnesses.

Close in prayer.

Acts 22:15
You will be his witness to all people of what you have seen and heard.

Going the Extra Mile

Activity

Use three large sheets of paper. At the top of one sheet, write "Jesus Is." On the second sheet, write "Jesus Said." On the remaining sheet, write "Jesus Did." Attach each sheet of paper to a wall. Help students form groups of three to six. Pass out markers or crayons to each group.

In your groups, think of something Jesus is, Jesus said, and Jesus did. Write the things you think of on the sheets of paper around the room. See how many different things you can write on each paper. If needed, explain the activity by saying, **For example, you might write "loving" on the paper that says "Jesus Is." You might write "Love your enemies" on the paper that says "Jesus Said," and you might write "died on the cross" on the paper that says "Jesus Did."** Allow time for students to complete the task. At the end of the activity, have students take turns reading aloud what is written on each of the sheets. **The things we have written will help us remember the good news we can say to others when we speak as witnesses for Jesus.**

Bible Discussion

Philip was a follower of Jesus and went to many towns telling people about Jesus. One day, Philip met an Ethiopian man who was reading the book of Isaiah. Let's read the story to see what happened next. Have a student read Acts 8:30–31, 34–35 aloud.

- **What did Philip do to be a witness for Jesus?**
- **What good news do you know about Jesus?**
- **Who has helped you learn good news about Jesus? Who can you tell about Jesus?**

Life Challenge

Philip was ready to speak about Jesus when the Ethiopian asked questions about Him. We can be ready to speak about Jesus to others too. Let's ask Jesus to help us be prepared to speak about Him.

Prayer

Lord Jesus, thank You for choosing us to tell others about Your love. Help us to be ready to speak to others about You. In Jesus' name. Amen.

Behind the Scenes

We can thank God for people who show His love by serving others.

Bible Talk

I need two volunteers to help with this activity. Position the volunteers as shown in the sketch. **As you listen to my story, the person in front can make facial expressions that go along with the story. The person in back moves the arms of the person in front to show the action of the story.**

Here's the story: One day I decided to go for a walk. Suddenly, a dog began to chase me! I was afraid and ran as fast as I could. I waved my hands at the dog to make him go away. Finally I couldn't see the dog anymore, so I kept walking. Now I was so hot and tired that I needed a drink of water. I bought an ice-cold bottle of water. I drank it very fast and started to walk home. But the same dog started chasing me again! This time I was really scared. I ran as fast as I could to get home. I quickly took my keys out my pocket as I was running. When I reached home, I frantically opened the door and slammed it shut. Whew! Next time I'll ask my mom to drive me.

Thank the volunteers for their help in telling the story.

- **Which of the two volunteers did the most work during the story?**
- **Which volunteer could you see the best?**

Believe it or not, there are people in our church who are kind of like _____ (name of student who was in the back). **They do a lot of work to make good things happen and show God's love, but they are rarely seen.**

Conclusion

We can thank God and pray for those people God uses behind the scenes to make our lives better.

Close in prayer.

Colossians 1:3

We always thank God, the Father of our Lord Jesus Christ, when we pray for you.

Going the Extra Mile

Activity

Pass out paper and markers to each student. *(Optional: Also provide a variety of decorating materials and glue sticks.)* **There are people in our church who work very hard to serve others. Today we're going to create thank-you cards to show our appreciation to the people in our church who make our lives better.** Allow 10 to 15 minutes for children to create their cards. Allow several volunteers to show their cards to the class and tell who the card was created for. **Wonderful job! It's always good to appreciate others.**

Bible Discussion

Have a student read 1 Thessalonians 5:11–13 aloud.

- **Why do you think the author of these verses wants us to encourage one another?**
- **What does the author of these verses say we should do for people who work hard among us?**

Paul, the author of these verses in the Bible, knew there were many people who went unnoticed, in spite of serving others to the best of their abilities. But these people never went unnoticed by God. He always sees those who are serving others, and we can thank God for that!

Life Challenge

Every day we probably walk right by people who are using their abilities to help others. Be ready to give them a well-deserved thank-you!

Prayer

Dear Lord, thank You for the people in our church who share Your love with us. Please help us take the time to thank them. In Jesus' name. Amen.

Enjoy Today

Be thankful for and enjoy what God has given you.

Bible Talk

Do you ever think it would be exciting to be all grown up? Let's see what kinds of things we could do if we were older. I would like each of you to silently act out what you would do if you were 20 years old. Allow a few minutes for students to pantomime actions. Describe the actions you see children acting out. **Perhaps you're looking forward to being old enough to drive a car. Maybe you can't wait to get a more difficult video game or a cool new skateboard.**

It's fun to look forward to doing things in the future. But sometimes we spend so much time wishing for the future that we forget to stop and enjoy the good things we can do right now—today!

In 1 Thessalonians 5:18, the Bible says, "Give thanks in all circumstances." This verse means that no matter what age we are, we can thank God for the things He has already given to us and allowed us to do. We don't have to spend a lot of time wanting things others have or wanting to do what others get to do.

Conclusion

Think about something you are glad you get to do today. Thank God for it—and enjoy it!

Close in prayer.

1 Thessalonians 5:18
Give thanks in all circumstances.

Going the Extra Mile

Activity

Give each student a pencil or marker and a sheet of paper. **I would like each of you to draw a time line of your life. First draw a line across the middle of your sheet of paper.** Demonstrate to students how to make the time line. **Draw an X at the beginning of the line that shows when you were born. Then think of three or four things you've learned to do from that time until now. Draw pictures or write what you've learned to do—and write how old you were when you learned those things.** Allow 10 to 15 minutes to complete the task. Invite a few students to share their time lines with the group. **Those time lines are wonderful! It's fun to look back at our lives to see how much we've learned and the good things God has helped us do.**

Bible Discussion

One of Jesus' followers wrote about how we can think about the future. Have a student read James 4:13–15 aloud.

- **How does James describe our lives in these verses?**
- **What is the main thing we can learn from these verses?**

James, a follower of Jesus and the author of these verses, explains to us that we should not brag about what will happen to us tomorrow or any day in the future. We can be thankful and enjoy today because we don't know for sure what will happen tomorrow. We do know that God will always be with us to help us and provide for us.

Life Challenge

God wants us to plan for the future but at the same time remember to enjoy our families, our church, and our friends every time we see them. Thank God for today!

Prayer

Lord, thank You for everything that You have given to us. Help us to enjoy Your good gifts every day. In Jesus' name. Amen.

The Secret of Contentment

God wants us to discover the secret of contentment so we can be thankful for the good things in our lives.

Bible Talk

It's fun to hear or discover a secret. A secret I like to hear is where someone has hidden some candy! Think of a secret you would like to hear or discover. Maybe you'd like to know the secret of what your birthday present is going to be or where your family is going to go on vacation. Pause briefly to allow each student to think of a secret. **Now stand up and whisper your secret to at least two other people.** After children have completed the activity, have volunteers tell what secrets they would like to hear or discover.

The Bible tells us about a secret we can all discover. Paul, a follower of God, says in Philippians 4:12, "I have learned the secret of being content in any and every situation." Paul had discovered the secret of being content no matter how little or how much he had. Instead of spending lots of time wishing for more and more things, Paul was thankful for the good things he had.

Conclusion

We like to think about things we'd like to have, but every day we can have a secret: being content and thankful for what God has given us.

Close in prayer.

Philippians 4:12

I have learned the secret of being content in any and every situation.

Going the Extra Mile

Activity

Help students form groups of three to six. Give each group several sheets of paper and a pencil. **Are you ready for a challenge? In your groups, you have 20 seconds to write down as many different things as you can that you are glad you have. Have you thought of something? Choose one person in your group to write down your ideas. Ready, set, go!** Use a timer to count off approximately 20 seconds, and then call time. Groups should count the items on their lists. Repeat the activity several more times, each time using new paper and increasing the time by ten seconds. For each round, remind students that they cannot duplicate items on their lists. After several rounds, each group counts the total number of items on their lists and tells some of the items from their lists.

If we really wrote down everything we're glad we have, our lists would probably be endless. Remembering the things on our lists can help us discover the secret of contentment and being thankful to God.

Bible Discussion

One reason we can be content is because we have an amazing promise from God. Have a student read Philippians 4:4–7, 10–13 aloud.

- **What promise from God did Paul write about in these verses?**
- **What did Paul say we should do when we are anxious or worried about anything?**
- **When is a time a kid your age might want to pray to God about worries or needs?**

Paul wrote these words when he was in prison, even though he had done nothing wrong. He had discovered the secret of contentment and being thankful, even when he was in prison and not free to do what he wanted. Paul told us about his joyful feelings and the way he relied on Jesus for strength to handle anything that happened.

Life Challenge

It's not wrong to think about more or better things we wish we had, but we can always remember to let God know what we need and then thank Him for what He has already given us. Remember that because of God's love, we've discovered the secret of being content and thankful! Praise God for His good gifts!

Prayer

Lord, we praise You for Your love and for the good things You've given us. Remind us every day to be content and to thank You. In Jesus' name. Amen.

Scripture Index

Old Testament

New Testament